T0183298

Lecture Notes in Computer Science   12411

Founding Editors

Gerhard Goos
Karlsruhe Institute of Technology, Karlsruhe, Germany
Juris Hartmanis
Cornell University, Ithaca, NY, USA

Editorial Board Members

Elisa Bertino
Purdue University, West Lafayette, IN, USA
Wen Gao
Peking University, Beijing, China
Bernhard Steffen◉
TU Dortmund University, Dortmund, Germany
Gerhard Woeginger◉
RWTH Aachen, Aachen, Germany
Moti Yung
Columbia University, New York, NY, USA

More information about this series at http://www.springer.com/series/7408

Joao Eduardo Ferreira · Balaji Palanisamy ·
Kejiang Ye · Siva Kantamneni ·
Liang-Jie Zhang (Eds.)

Services – SERVICES 2020

16th World Congress
Held as Part of the Services Conference Federation, SCF 2020
Honolulu, HI, USA, September 18–20, 2020
Proceedings

 Springer

Editors
Joao Eduardo Ferreira ⓘ
University of Sao Paulo
São Paulo, Brazil

Balaji Palanisamy
University of Pittsburgh
Pittsburgh, PA, USA

Kejiang Ye
Shenzhen Institutes of Advanced
Technology, Chinese Academy of Sciences
Shenzhen, China

Siva Kantamneni ⓘ
Deloitte Consulting
New York, NY, USA

Liang-Jie Zhang ⓘ
Kingdee International Software
Group Co., Ltd
Shenzhen, China

ISSN 0302-9743   ISSN 1611-3349 (electronic)
Lecture Notes in Computer Science
ISBN 978-3-030-59594-4   ISBN 978-3-030-59595-1 (eBook)
https://doi.org/10.1007/978-3-030-59595-1

LNCS Sublibrary: SL2 – Programming and Software Engineering

© Springer Nature Switzerland AG 2020
This work is subject to copyright. All rights are reserved by the Publisher, whether the whole or part of the material is concerned, specifically the rights of translation, reprinting, reuse of illustrations, recitation, broadcasting, reproduction on microfilms or in any other physical way, and transmission or information storage and retrieval, electronic adaptation, computer software, or by similar or dissimilar methodology now known or hereafter developed.
The use of general descriptive names, registered names, trademarks, service marks, etc. in this publication does not imply, even in the absence of a specific statement, that such names are exempt from the relevant protective laws and regulations and therefore free for general use.
The publisher, the authors and the editors are safe to assume that the advice and information in this book are believed to be true and accurate at the date of publication. Neither the publisher nor the authors or the editors give a warranty, expressed or implied, with respect to the material contained herein or for any errors or omissions that may have been made. The publisher remains neutral with regard to jurisdictional claims in published maps and institutional affiliations.

This Springer imprint is published by the registered company Springer Nature Switzerland AG
The registered company address is: Gewerbestrasse 11, 6330 Cham, Switzerland

Preface

The World Congress on Services (SERVICES 2020) aims to provide an international forum to attract researchers, practitioners, and industry business leaders in all the following services sectors to help define and shape the modernization strategy and directions of the services industry.

This volume presents the accepted papers of SERVICES 2020, held as a fully virtual conference during September 18–20, 2020. All topics regard software engineering foundations and applications, with a focus on novel approaches for engineering requirements, design and architectures, testing, maintenance and evolution, model-driven development, software processes, metrics, quality assurance and new software economics models, search-based software engineering, benefiting day-to-day services sectors and derived through experiences, with appreciation to scale, pragmatism, transparency, compliance, and/or dependability.

We accepted nine papers, including five full papers and four short papers. Each was reviewed and selected by at least three independent members of the SERVICES 2020 International Program Committee. We are pleased to thank the authors whose submissions and participation made this conference possible. We also want to express our thanks to the Program Committee members, for their dedication in helping to organize the conference and reviewing the submissions. We owe special thanks to the keynote speakers for their impressive speeches.

July 2020

Joao Eduardo Ferreira
Balaji Palanisamy
Kejiang Ye
Siva Kantamneni
Liang-Jie Zhang

Organization

General Chair

Jamal Bentahar   Concordia University, Canada

Program Chairs

Joao Eduardo Ferreira	University of Sao Paulo, Brazil
Balaji Palanisamy	University of Pittsburgh, USA
Kejiang Ye (Vice-chair)	Shenzhen Institutes of Advanced Technology, Chinese Academy of Sciences, China
Siva Kantamneni (Vice-chair)	Deloitte Consulting, USA
Liang-Jie Zhang	Kingdee International Software Group Co., Ltd, China

Services Conference Federation (SCF 2020)

General Chairs

Yi Pan	Georgia State University, USA
Samee U. Khan	North Dakota State University, USA
Wu Chou	Essenlix Corporation, USA
Ali Arsanjani	Amazon Web Services (AWS), USA

Program Chair

Liang-Jie Zhang   Kingdee International Software Group Co., Ltd, China

Industry Track Chair

Siva Kantamneni   Deloitte Consulting, USA

CFO

Min Luo   Georgia Tech, USA

Industry Exhibit and International Affairs Chair

Zhixiong Chen   Mercy College, USA

Operation Committee

Jing Zeng	Yundee Intelligence Co., Ltd, China
Yishuang Ning	Tsinghua University, China

| Sheng He | Tsinghua University, China |
| Yang Liu | Tsinghua University, China |

Steering Committee

| Calton Pu (Co-chair) | Georgia Tech, USA |
| Liang-Jie Zhang (Co-chair) | Kingdee International Software Group Co., Ltd, China |

SERVICES 2020 Program Committee

Xiuhua Li	Chongqing University, China
Xin Luo	Chongqing Institute of Green and Intelligent Technology, China
Stefano Sebastio	Inria Rennes, France

Conference Sponsor – Services Society

Services Society (S2) is a nonprofit professional organization that has been created to promote worldwide research and technical collaboration in services innovation among academia and industrial professionals. Its members are volunteers from industry and academia with common interests. S2 is registered in the USA as a "501(c) organization," which means that it is an American tax-exempt nonprofit organization. S2 collaborates with other professional organizations to sponsor or co-sponsor conferences and to promote an effective services curriculum in colleges and universities. The S2 initiates and promotes a "Services University" program worldwide to bridge the gap between industrial needs and university instruction.

The services sector accounted for 79.5% of the USA's GDP in 2016. The world's most service-oriented economy, with service sectors accounting for more than 90% of the GDP. S2 has formed 10 Special Interest Groups (SIGs) to support technology and domain specific professional activities:

- Special Interest Group on Web Services (SIG-WS)
- Special Interest Group on Services Computing (SIG-SC)
- Special Interest Group on Services Industry (SIG-SI)
- Special Interest Group on Big Data (SIG-BD)
- Special Interest Group on Cloud Computing (SIG-CLOUD)
- Special Interest Group on Artificial Intelligence (SIG-AI)
- Special Interest Group on Edge Computing (SIG-EC)
- Special Interest Group on Cognitive Computing (SIG-CC)
- Special Interest Group on Blockchain (SIG-BC)
- Special Interest Group on Internet of Things (SIG-IOT)

About the Services Conference Federation (SCF)

As the founding member of the Services Conference Federation (SCF), the First International Conference on Web Services (ICWS 2003) was held in June 2003 in Las Vegas, USA. Meanwhile, the First International Conference on Web Services - Europe 2003 (ICWS-Europe 2003) was held in Germany in October 2003. ICWS-Europe 2003 was is an extended event of ICWS 2003, and held in Europe. In 2004, ICWS-Europe was changed to the European Conference on Web Services (ECOWS), which was held in Erfurt, Germany. SCF 2019 was held successfully in San Diego, USA. To celebrate its 18th birthday, SCF 2020 was held virtually during September 18–20, 2020.

In the past 17 years, the ICWS community has expanded from Web engineering innovations to scientific research for the whole services industry. The service delivery platforms have been expanded to mobile platforms, Internet of Things (IoT), cloud computing, and edge computing. The service's ecosystem is gradually enabled, value added, and intelligence embedded through enabling technologies such as big data, artificial intelligence (AI), and cognitive computing. In the coming years, all the transactions with multiple parties involved will be transformed to blockchain.

Based on the technology trends and best practices in the field, SCF will continue serving as the conference umbrella's code name for all service-related conferences. SCF 2020 defines the future of New ABCDE (AI, Blockchain, Cloud, big Data, Everything is connected), which enable IoT and enter the 5G for the Services Era. SCF 2020's 10 collocated theme topic conferences all center around "services," while each focusing on exploring different themes (web-based services, cloud-based services, big data-based services, services innovation lifecycle, AI-driven ubiquitous services, blockchain driven trust service-ecosystems, industry-specific services and applications, and emerging service-oriented technologies). SCF includes 10 service-oriented conferences: ICWS, CLOUD, SCC, BigData Congress, AIMS, SERVICES, ICIOT, EDGE, ICCC, and ICBC. The SCF 2020 members are listed as follows:

[1] The International Conference on Web Services (ICWS 2020, http://icws.org/) is the flagship theme-topic conference for Web-based services, featuring Web services modeling, development, publishing, discovery, composition, testing, adaptation, delivery, as well as the latest API standards.

[2] The International Conference on Cloud Computing (CLOUD 2020, http://thecloudcomputing.org/) is the flagship theme-topic conference for modeling, developing, publishing, monitoring, managing, delivering XaaS (Everything as a Service) in the context of various types of cloud environments.

[3] The International Conference on Big Data (BigData 2020, http://bigdatacongress.org/) is the emerging theme-topic conference for the scientific and engineering innovations of big data.

[4] The International Conference on Services Computing (SCC 2020, http://thescc.org/) is the flagship theme-topic conference for services innovation lifecycle that includes enterprise modeling, business consulting, solution creation, services

orchestration, services optimization, services management, services marketing, and business process integration and management.

[5]   The International Conference on AI & Mobile Services (AIMS 2020, http://ai1000.org/) is the emerging theme-topic conference for the science and technology of AI, and the development, publication, discovery, orchestration, invocation, testing, delivery, and certification of AI-enabled services and mobile applications.

[6]   The World Congress on Services (SERVICES 2020, http://servicescongress.org/) focuses on emerging service-oriented technologies and the industry-specific services and solutions.

[7]   The International Conference on Cognitive Computing (ICCC 2020, http://thecognitivecomputing.org/) focuses on the Sensing Intelligence (SI) as a Service (SIaaS) which makes systems listen, speak, see, smell, taste, understand, interact, and walk in the context of scientific research and engineering solutions.

[8]   The International Conference on Internet of Things (ICIOT 2020, http://iciot.org/) focuses on the creation of IoT technologies and development of IOT services.

[9]   The International Conference on Edge Computing (EDGE 2020, http://theedgecomputing.org/) focuses on the state of the art and practice of edge computing including but not limited to localized resource sharing, connections with the cloud, and 5G devices and applications.

[10]   The International Conference on Blockchain (ICBC 2020, http://blockchain1000.org/) concentrates on blockchain-based services and enabling technologies.

Some highlights of SCF 2020 are shown below:

–   **Bigger Platform:** The 10 collocated conferences (SCF 2020) are sponsored by the Services Society (S2) which is the world-leading nonprofit organization (501 c(3)) dedicated to serving more than 30,000 worldwide services computing researchers and practitioners. Bigger platform means bigger opportunities to all volunteers, authors, and participants. Meanwhile, Springer sponsors the Best Paper Awards and other professional activities. All the 10 conference proceedings of SCF 2020 have been published by Springer and indexed in ISI Conference Proceedings Citation Index (included in Web of Science), Engineering Index EI (Compendex and Inspec databases), DBLP, Google Scholar, IO-Port, MathSciNet, Scopus, and ZBlMath.

–   **Brighter Future:** While celebrating the 2020 version of ICWS, SCF 2020 highlights the Third International Conference on Blockchain (ICBC 2020) to build the fundamental infrastructure for enabling secure and trusted service ecosystems. It will also lead our community members to create their own brighter future.

–   **Better Model:** SCF 2020 continues to leverage the invented Conference Blockchain Model (CBM) to innovate the organizing practices for all the 10 theme conferences.

Contents

Case Study on Key Influencing Factors of Modern Service Industry Development

Zhu Xiangbo[1,2(✉)], Ou Guoliang[1], Li Yi[3], and Zhou Zhigang[1]

[1] Shenzhen Polytechnic, Shenzhen 518055, Guangdong, People's Republic of China
zxb@szpt.edu.cn
[2] China Three Gorges University, Yichang 443002, Hubei, People's Republic of China
[3] Shenzhen Institute of Information Technology, Shenzhen 518172, Guangdong, People's Republic of China

Abstract. In the process of industrial structure adjustment and economic development model innovation, the role and status of modern service industry are becoming increasingly important. Shenzhen Municipal People's Government had paid great attention on the development of modern service industry. On one hand, modern service industry has been quite large and mature, and on the other hand, there are problems of insufficient in total volume, relatively narrow industry field and somehow inadequate industry structure. Based on rational choosing and building an influencing indicator system, this paper tries to analysis the development of modern service industry in Shenzhen. Through using methods such as cointegration analysis, Granger causality test and multiple linear regression, combined with the relevant data collected, we found that the foreign direct investment and the investment level of modern service industry are the key factors. Therefore, this paper suggested that the development of modern service industry in Shenzhen might improve on expanding foreign investment, strengthening the investment level of modern service industry, and upgrading professional talents.

Keywords: Modern service industry · Influencing factors · Multi-Regression analysis

1 Introduction

The modern service industry is a service industry that maintains the continuity of the industrial production process, promotes industrial technological progress and industrial upgrading, and improves production efficiency to provide guarantee services. It is the result of heightened industrial structure and economic service.

In the background of the continuous deepening of the industrial structure adjustment and economic development model innovation in Shenzhen, the role and status of the modern service industry are becoming increasingly important. Shenzhen Municipal People's Government had formulate policies to strengthen the development of modern service industry. As early as 2007, "Several opinions on accelerating the development of our city's high-end service industry" had been put forward. In 2012 and 2017,

© Springer Nature Switzerland AG 2020
J. E. Ferreira et al. (Eds.): SERVICES 2020, LNCS 12411, pp. 1–10, 2020.
https://doi.org/10.1007/978-3-030-59595-1_1

"The 12th Five-Year Plan for the Development of Modern Service Industry in Shenzhen" and "The 13th Five-Year Plan for the Development of Modern Service Industry in Shenzhen" came out. In 2018, "Shenzhen Strategic Emerging Industries Development Special Fund Support Policy" was carried out to support the Strategic Emerging Industries. In 2019, the added value of modern service industry was 1,210.147 billion yuan, an increase of 12% with last year. Among them, the operating income of information transmission, software and information technology services increased by 16.5%, transportation, warehousing and postal services increased by 9.1%, leasing and business services increased by 11.2%, and scientific research and technical services increased by 11.9%.

From the perspective of development direction, the application of technologies and concepts in Shenzhen, such as cross-border finance, factor markets, wealth management, supply chain management, e-commerce logistics, and the internet of things have transformed the modern service industry into a high-tech and high-value-added high-end direction. However, the modern service industry in Shenzhen has problems such as insufficient in total volume, relatively narrow industry field, and insufficient employment potential. It also faces many difficulties such as insufficient internal structure optimization, severe factor constraints, and high competitive pressure. It is the primary issues if Shenzhen Municipal People's Government wants to effectively improve the modern service industry system, achieve the optimization and upgrading of industrial structure and clarify the key factors affecting.

2 Literature Review

2.1 Concepts and Characteristics of Modern Service Industry

Modern service industry appears with the concepts of "knowledge-intensive service industry", "emerging service industry" and "production service industry". It is characterized by knowledge-based, highly R & D-intensive and high value-added knowledge. Wang X Q et al. (2011) analyzed the modern service industry in the United States, Japan and Singapore and divided the modern service industry into three types, such as a native type, an embedded type and an exogenous type [1]. Wu X B et al. (2014) used the data from China's GEM modern service industry and cluster analysis method, and then found that the modern service industry had six typical business models [2]. According to the National Development and Reform Commission's "Industrial Structure Adjustment Guidance Catalogue"(2019, Exposure Draft), the modern service industry includes following nine major industries: (1) information transmission, computer services and software industry; (2) financial industry (3) real estate; (4) leasing and business services; (5) scientific research, technical services and geological exploration; (6) water conservancy, environment and public facilities management; (7) education; (8) Health, social security and social services; (9) culture, sports and entertainment.

2.2 Influencing Factors of Modern Service Industry

For the interaction between modern service industry and other industries, some scholars put forward their opinions. Based on the review of the development of modern service industry in Wuhan, Kuang Y F (2015) found that the development of modern service industry could effectively promote the transformation and upgrading of industrial structure, and then promote regional economic growth [3]. Li J M et al. (2013) believed that the development of modern service industry was a necessary condition for economic structure optimization and adjustment [4].

For the influencing factors, different scholars used different methods and found differentiated indicators. Hou S G (2014) comprehensively analyzed the nine influencing factors of modern service industry and found that the impact of industrial structure was the most significant [5]. Liu T (2010) used multiple regression model to examine the influencing factors of the development and changes of modern service industry in Hunan Province, and found that the output value of modern service industry were related to per capita GDP and disposable income of urban residents, and the latter two variables had negative impact on the former one [6]. Through combined with the data of modern service industry development in some provinces and used multi-factor analysis model, Ma F H (2016) pointed out that economic growth and urbanization process, residents' consumption and government expenditure all significantly affected the development of modern service industry [7]. With using multiple linear regression method and data from China's modern service industry in 2010, Li D M (2011) verified that per capita disposable income was a decisive factor affecting the development of modern service industry [8]. Mao Y Y (2010) divided the factors that affecting the development of modern service industry into tangible and intangible aspects. The tangible factors included infrastructure conditions, urbanization level, consumption demand, government related policies and secondary industry development status, while the intangible factors were mainly including external economic influence, labor cost and marketization degree [9]. Taking into account the knowledge of the modern service industry, Li J (2010) summarized the factors as residents' consumption status, overall economic development level, information level, industrialization level, urbanization level and internationalization level [10]. Zeng X F et al. (2013) studied the influencing factors of the regional service industry, and concluded that the basic knowledge structure, technological environment, social environment and technological support were the main factors affecting the development of modern service industry [11]. Through empirical analysis, Bai J (2018) found that foreign investment, urbanization, and government spending had a positive impact on the competitiveness of modern service industries [12]. Wang M K (2017) used principal component regression analysis and found that factors such as industrialization rate, GDP per capita, number of employees in the service industry, and actual use of foreign capital affected the improvement of the competitiveness of the service industry [13]. Using partial least squares regression analysis and data collected from Henan Province, Tian ZZ (2019) found that the level of urbanization, information, government role, innovation capability and economic development had a significant impact on the development of producer services [14]. Based on the perspective of "added value-participation-division of labor", Zheng G J et al. (2018) studied the competitiveness of the service industry, research results showed that the division of labor in the global value chain of the service industry and the international division of labor participation were the most important and the most Significant factors [15]. By selecting explanatory variables such as manufacturing agglomeration, government protection, urbanization level, human capital, and information level, and used spatial constant coefficient models, Zheng C J et al. (2017) analyzed the influencing factors of knowledge-intensive service industry development in Zhejiang Province [16]. Through an empirical analysis, Hong W Y (2015) found that the factors affecting the international competitiveness of the high-tech service industry in China and the United States included the number of high-tech service industry employees, the level of residents 'consumption, the level of residents' consumption, and the amount of investment in fixed assets in the high-tech service industry [17].

2.3 Evaluation and Empirical Research on the Development of Modern Service Industry

Shen X P (2012) comprehensively introduced the composition and characteristics, development environment and basic conditions of Shenzhen's modern service industry. Through the application of modern service industry added value as a percentage of GDP, growth contribution rate, economic growth driving force and other factors, the contribution of modern service industry to Shenzhen's economic growth was discussed, and its future development in terms of development goals and key areas were prospected [18]. Zhang H M et al. (2018) measured service industry development level in the Guangdong-Hong Kong-Macao Greater Bay Area. By using indicators such as rationalization of service industry structure, industry efficiency level and service industry structure heightening, and GMM model, the causality between the service industry development level in the Bay Area and the coordination level of cities [19]. Wu J X (2019) proposed relevant evaluation indicators based on the Porter Diamond Model and analyzed the competitiveness of China's science and technology service industry using an analytic hierarchy process [20]. Kang J et al. (2015) used principal component analysis to compare the competitiveness of the service industry in three different stages of cities in the Yangtze River Delta [21]. Zhang S J et al. (2016) used the annual data of the "BRICS" from 2009 to 2013, and factor analysis method to compare the international competitiveness of service industries [22]. Wang Y et al. (2018) explored the service industry development level of provinces and regions along the "Belt and Road" in China using factor analysis [23].

2.4 Comments

In general, the study on modern service industry is quiet mature, and the empirical researches using various data and methods are abundant. For example, in the influencing factors and evaluation research of modern service industry development, various indicators such as residents' consumption status, overall economic development level, information level, industrialization level, per capita GDP and disposable income of urban residents, etc., had constructed for analysis from different angles. However, the model setting and indicator system construction have not unified yet. At the same time, there is relatively little research focused on Shenzhen. Based on this, in order to promote Shenzhen's modern service industry development and put forward corresponding countermeasures and suggestions, this article intends to take Shenzhen's modern service industry as the object, select the latest and detailed data, and discuss its development status and key influencing factors.

3 Influencing Factor Model and Index of Modern Service Industry Development

3.1 Construction of Influencing Factor Index

From the "Diamond Model" put forward by Michael Porter, the international competitiveness of an industry mainly depends on four key factors and two auxiliary factors. Four key factors include demand conditions (driving force), factor conditions (human resources, knowledge resources, capital and other factors), related and supporting industries (strongly supported), corporate strategy, institutions, and competitors. While two auxiliary factors are the government and opportunities. Four key factors and two auxiliary factors jointly affect the industrial development and competitiveness. Together with the results of Mao YY (2010) and Wang J (2018), the factors that influencing the development of modern service industry can be subdivided into tangible factors and intangible factors [9, 12]. Tangible factors mainly refer to factors with material form, including capital investment, technological improvement, and infrastructure construction. Intangible factors are mainly factors with no specific form, including personnel literacy, consumption level, and government philosophy and so on. According to the attributes of modern service industry, and by summarizing the aforementioned research, the following indicator system is constructed. The value added of modern service industry (MSVA) represents the development level of modern service industry Table 1.

3.2 Descriptive Statistics

The original data is collected from the Shenzhen Statistical Yearbook and related statistical bulletins (2001-2020), and some scattered ones are compiled from the website of the Statistics Bureau. For all variables, value are collected from 2000 to 2019, which last twenty years. The value added of modern service industry (MSVA) acted as the dependent variable of the evaluation model. Other influencing factors treated as independent variables. Through logarithmic processing all variables, we use the logarithmic value of them Table 2.

3.3 Stationarity Test, Cointegration Test and Granger Causality Test

For time series data, the stationarity test is an indispensable link. The co-integration test is to verify whether there is a co-integration relationship between those influencing factors as independent variables and modern service industry development level as dependent variables, before performing multiple regression analysis. While granger causality test is to verify whether each factor has a correlation with the dependent variable, and it can clearly verify which variable caused the change of which variable.

Stationarity Test. Using ADF method to check the stationarity of time series. Result showed the difference in the dimensions get the significant result, which means that these variables are all second-order single integers. Result of the unit root test can found in the following table:

Table 1. Indicator system of modern service industry development

Type	Name	Content	Calculation method
Tangible factors	Modern Service Industry Investment Level (MSII)	Modern service industry investment status indicator	The proportion of service industry fixed asset investment in total investment
	Population density (PD)	Urbanization rate indicator	Urban population density
	Foreign direct investment (FDI)	Opening up indicator	Actual use of foreign capital
	Employees in modern service industry (PEMS)	Labor indicator	Number of employees in modern service industry
Intangible factor	Total retail sales of consumer goods per capita (PTRS)	Spending power indicator	Total retail sales of consumer goods per capita
	Per capita general public budget income (CPBI)	Government fiscal level indicator	Per capita general public budget income
	Per capita disposable income (PDGI)	Income level indicator	Per capita disposable income
	GDP per capita (CGDP)	City development level indicator	GDP per capita

From the table above, it can easily find that Lncgdp is stable in the level, while the Lnptrs and Lncpbi are not stable in the level and in the difference. After the difference, other variables are stable and are second-order single integers Table 3.

Cointegration Test. Results of unit root test show that Lnmsva and Lnpdgi, Lnmsii, Lnpd, Lncgdp, Lnfdi and Lnpems are all second-order single integers, and there may be a long-term equilibrium relationship between variables. Since it is a multivariate cointegration adjustment, we applied the Johansen test to inspect the cointegration relationship among them. Co-integration results proved that the co-integration rank of the stationary variable (Lnpdgi, Lnmsii, Lnpd, Lncgdp, Lnfdi and Lnpems) are all 1. That is, these six variable and Lnmsva exist separately and there is only one cointegration relationship. In addition, from the value of each cointegration parameter vector, Lnpdgi, Lnmsii, Lnpd, Lncgdp, Lnfdi and Lnpems have a long-term equilibrium relationship with the vector Lnmsva.

Granger Causality Test. The results of the cointegration test prove that there is a correlation between the selected variables and dependent variable. It is not clear who caused the specific variables and the dependent variable. Then, use the Granger causality test method to check the influencing relationship between variables. After selecting the

Table 2. Descriptive statistics of indicators (logarithmic value, from 2000 to 2019)

Variable name (unit)	Average value	Standard deviation	Minimum value	Maximum value
Value Added of Modern Service Industry (MSVA)(100 million yuan)	4353.59	3532.24	607.84	12101.47
Per capita disposable income (PDGI)(10 thousand yuan)	35520.2	12753.68	21494.00	62252.00
Modern Service Industry Investment Level (MSII)(%)	77.14	5.7979	62.65	85.99
Population density (PD)(10 thousand people per square kilometers)	4953.03	986.82	3348.04	6727.91
GDP per capita (CGDP)(10 thousand yuan)	106446.5	55078.69	33276	193211
Foreign Direct Investment (FDI)(100 million yuan)	893.13	453.66	121.67	3653.48
Number of employees in modern service industry (PEMS)	145.49	72.31	52.56	299.1
Total retail sales of consumer goods per capita (PTRS)	30162.7	14235.42	11021	50013
Per capita disposable income (PDGI)	13178.25	9384.49	3328	9965

granger causality test with second-order lag, all the results begins to get the significance. Results showed that Lnpdgi, Lnmsii, Lnpd, Lncgdp, Lnfdi, Lnpems are the reason that affects the vector Lnmsva.

3.4 Multiple Linear Regression

Co-integration and Granger causality test that confirmed these important factors had significant influence on the development level of modern service industry, and showed the causal relationship between them, while the affecting size was not yet determined. Construct a multiple regression model and analyze each influencing factor and the development level of modern service industry. Choose the development level of modern service industry (Lnmsva) as the dependent variable, and other factors as independent variables Table 4.

Table 3. Results of unit root test

Test variable	ADF Test(P-Value)	Stationary
Lnmsva Dlnmsva	−0.990541(0.7346) **−3.133171(0.0411***)**	unstable **stable**
Lnpdgi Dlnpdgi	0.535625(0.9833) **−4.043027(0.0069****)**	unstable **stable**
Lnmsii Dlnmsii	−1.597686(0.4643) **−5.126838(0.0008*****)**	unstable **stable**
Lnpd Dlnpd	−1.703873(0.4095) **−3.564762(0.0180****)**	unstable **stable**
Lncgdp Dlncgdp	**−3.185447(0.037***)** −1.802981(0.3671)	**stable** unstable
Lnfdi Dlnfdi	−1.225460(0.6408) **−3.692236(0.0147****)**	unstable **stable**
Lnpems Dlnpems	−0.600491(0.8486) **−4.454073(0.0030****)**	unstable **stable**
Lnptrs Dlnptrs	−2.336485(0.1721) −1.788217(0.3737)	unstable unstable
Lncpbi Dlncpbi	−0.396755(0.8912) −2.557374(0.1196)	unstable unstable

Note: *, **, *** means significant at the confidence level of 10%, 5% and 1%

Table 4. Results of the multiple linear regression

Variable	C	Lnpdgi	Lnmsii	Lnpd	Lncgdp	Lnfdi	Lnpems
Coefficient	**−13.91283**** (0.0224)	**0.2949**** (0.02258)	**0.52758**** (0.0319)	0.9183 (0.2675)	**1.0709***** (0.0003)	**1.4206**** (0.0443)	0.3078 (0.3948)

Note: *, **, *** means significant at the confidence level of 10%, 5% and 1%

From the results of the regression equation, the regression-fitting coefficient R^2 is 0.9955, the F value is 485.59, the equation passes the significance test, and the multiple regression equation is valid. Factors such as the per capita disposable income of urban residents (Lnpdgi), the level of investment in modern services (Lnmsii), the level of GDP per capita (Lncgdp), and foreign direct investment (Lnfdi) have significantly affected the development of modern services (Lnmsva). Among them, the level of significance brought by GDP per capita is the best.

From the perspective of influence, all factors have a positive impact on the development level of modern service industry. In terms of impact level, foreign direct investment (Lnfdi) has the highest impact level. When foreign direct investment increases by 1 percentage point, the value added of the modern service industry increases by 1.42 percentage points. This followed by level of GDP per capita (Lncgdp), level of investment in modern services (Lnmsii), and level of per capita disposable income of urban residents (Lnpdgi), with coefficients of 1.0709, 0.5275, and 0.2949, respectively. When each variable increases by 1 percentage point, the level of modern service industry increases by 1.07, 0.52, and 0.29 percentage points, respectively.

4   Conclusion and Suggestion

The vigorous development of modern service industry in Shenzhen has promoted development and transformation of the social economy, and then become the engine of regional economic growth. However, it still faces related problems, such as weak growth and excessive dependence on a certain industry. At the same time, the impact of the new crown epidemic (NCP, COVID-19) this year has also challenged the pace of development in Shenzhen. Combining the above research, this article believes that:

Optimize the level and structure of foreign direct investment to better support the development of modern service industries. Use foreign direct investment to increase the investment level of modern service industry, thereby optimizing the development structure of modern service industry and upgrading the level and level of modern service industry in Shenzhen.

Promote the investment level and structure of government investment on service industry, and then support the high-quality development of modern service industry. Strengthen the leading role of government on the investment, then guide more and better capital invest into the modern service industry. Try to expand its fields and to optimize its structure, thus to build a more innovative and dynamic development pattern of the modern service industry.

Increase policy support for finance, taxation, capital and talents. From the aspect of talents, pay attention to improve the number and quality of employees in the modern service industry. In terms of finance and land, strengthen the expenditure of fiscal expenditure in the modern service industry.

Acknowledgements. This research was supported by Humanities and Social Sciences Annual Project of Shenzhen Polytechnic (No. 602930239, No. 2212s3080011), Innovative Engineering 2019 Annual Project of Shenzhen Polytechnic (No. cxgc2019b0004), Science and Technology Innovation Strategy Project 2020 Annual Project of Guangdong Province (No. pdjh2020b1185), Humanities and Social Sciences Youth Project of Hubei Provincial Department of Education (No. 17Q056), Soft Science research project of Hubei Provincial Department of Education (No. 2018ADC162), Open fund project of Hubei Provincial Humanities and Social Sciences Key Research Base–Reservoir Immigration Research Center (No. 2016KF11).

References

1. Wang, X., Liang, W.: Research on the aggregation model and its structure mechanism of modern service industry. Com. Res. **11**, 92–100 (2011)
2. Xiaobo, W., Yao Mingming, W., Dong, Z.: The classification of business model from the value network perspective: evidence from the modern service industry. J. Zhejiang Univ. Humanit. Soc. Sci. **2**, 64–77 (2014)
3. Kuang, Y.: An Empirical Study on the Relationship between Modern Service Industry, Industrial Structure and Economic Growth——Taking Wuhan as an Example, 1, 54–59 (2015)
4. Jianmin, L., Yuechun, C.: Research on the optimizing mechanism of modern service industry to industrial. Structure **9**, 10–16 (2013)
5. Hou Shouguo, D., Zifang, F.P.: Research on the development path of modern service industry based on principal component analysis. Stat. Dec. **7**, 140–142 (2014)
6. Ting, L., Jie, W.: An empirical study on the development of modern service industry in hunan province. Econ. Geogr. **3**, 466–471 (2010)
7. Fenghua, M.: Service industrial structure change in china: measures based on four dimensions. Econ. Manag. **2**, 26–33 (2016)

8. Daming, L., Quanzhang, X.: Research on the factors of regional differences in modern service industry development. J. Zhongnan Univ. Econ. Law **4**, 17–22 (2011)
9. Yuanyuan, M.: Research on the development status and influencing factors of modern service industry in jiangsu province. Yangzhou University, Yangzhou (2010)
10. Juan, L.: An analysis of the factors influencing the development of china's modern service industry. Comm. Res. **2**, 112–115 (2010)
11. Xiaofei, Z., Lvwei, X.: Research on influencing factors of knowledge-intensive service industry. Sci. Technol. Prog. Policy **30**, 53–56 (2013)
12. Bai, J.: Research on the Competitive Power and Influencing Factors of the Modern Service Industry in Jilin Province. Jilin University of Finance,Changchun (2018)
13. Wang, M.: Research on Hubei Province Service Industry Competitiveness and Its Influencing Factors. Huazhong University of Agriculture, Wuhan (2017)
14. Zhenzhong, T.: An empirical study on the influencing factors of the development of producer services. Stat. Dec. **35**, 112–115 (2019)
15. Guojiao, Z., Chunrong, Y.: A re-examination of the competitiveness of china's service industry and its influencing factors-based on the perspective of "value-added-participation-division of labor". Econ. Vis. **2**, 17–18 (2018)
16. Joanna. Competitiveness in International Trade in Knowledge-Intensive Services–The Case of Poland, Comparative Economic Research, 17, 75–89 (2014)
17. Hong, W.: Comparative Study on the International Competitiveness of Chinese and American High-tech Service Industry and Its Influencing Factors, Hefei. Anhui University of Finance (2015)
18. Shen, X., Tan, L., Xiao, C., Gong, J.: Report of Shenzhen Economic Development, Beijing: Social Sciences Academic Press, pp. 177–187 (2012)
19. Zhong, Y., Hu, X.: The construction and system innovation of the Guangdong-Hong Kong-Macao greater bay area: theoretical basis and implementation mechanism. Economist **12**, 50–57 (2017)
20. Gai, K., Yuming, S., Kun, L.: The evaluation and spatial-temporal evolution of urban service industry competitiveness in yangtze river economic region. J. Sichuan Norm. Univ. Nat. Sci. **3**, 452–459 (2015)
21. Grover, A.G., Sebastian, S.: Trade in services competitiveness: an assessment methodology. J. Int. Comm. Econ. Policy **5**, 120–136 (2014)
22. Shaojie, Z., Hong, L.: The comparative evaluation study of international competitiveness of service industry in BRICS. China Soft Sci. **1**, 154–164 (2016)
23. Wang, Y., Weijin Suntao, Z.: Study on the development and optimization of regional service industry under the background of B & R initiative. China Soft Sci. **5**, 101–109 (2018)

Blockchain Driven Three Domain Secure 2.x in Digital Payment Services Architecture

Vikas S. Shah[✉]

Knights of Columbus, New Haven, CT 06510, USA
shah_vikas_s@usa.net

Abstract. Due to the recent advancements in digital commerce, consumers expect real-time digital payment convenient and available across channels as more connected devices become payment devices. It offers consumers to pay in-store or online purchases in many diversified ways. The three domains secure protocol evolved to version 2.x (3DS2) supporting the development in digital payment domain and its rapid adaptation. The specification includes the provisioning of the application-based purchases enabling risk-based decisions to authenticate the consumer transactions. 3DS2 enhances consumers' checkout experiences through out-of-band authentication. It eliminates the need for enrollment process and static password supporting non-payment activities and native mobile. The primary challenges to implement 3DS2 are dimensioning the risks, real-time variability in the risk factors, and precision to compute the accumulative risk associated with the individuals. Financial services, merchants, and consumers are enabled to connect into the blockchain network using application programming interfaces (APIs). It alleviates participants of Blockchain network from having to build out their own distributed transactions' server nodes. This paper proposes a blockchain-driven 3DS2 service architecture framework that integrates the risk-based decisions and provides a secure communication platform in digital commerce. We illustrate the increased level of authenticity, maintainability, extendibility, and flexibility in the digital payment ecosystem with the industry case study of membership-based in-store or online charitable contribution campaigns during point-of-sale.

Keywords: Application programming interface (API) · Blockchain (BC) · Digital activity (DA) · Frictionless flow · Risk factor (RF) · Three domain secure 2.x (3DS2)

1 Introduction

In 2019, the online fraudulent transactions increased to 27% and 42% consumers experienced the unauthorized payment activities [1]. The results impacted entire supply-chain, including delays in shipments, consumer traffic, and in-store purchases. Survey of 166 United States' merchant conducted by Federal Reserve Bank of Minneapolis indicates that the Card Not Present (CNP) is the top payment threat to retailers [2]. The Nilson Report announced the losses from worldwide fraud on credit cards, debit cards and pre-paid cards hit $27.85 billion last year on a total card sales volume of $40.582 trillion [3].

© Springer Nature Switzerland AG 2020
J. E. Ferreira et al. (Eds.): SERVICES 2020, LNCS 12411, pp. 11–27, 2020.
https://doi.org/10.1007/978-3-030-59595-1_2

The Merchants pay up to 3.5% in the transaction fees. Besides, merchants are subject to flat fees for point-of-sale terminal usage, network charges, and incidental expenses such as chargebacks in case of fraud or disputes. Every dollar of fraud now costs banks and credit unions about $2.92, a 9.3% increase over 2017. The payment industry has seen enough data breaches to affect at least a few billion people across the globe.

The merchants, retailers, consumers, and issuers are always in the exploration of approaches to reduce payments fraud in the digital business ecosystem effectively. According to statistics presented in [4], the average active connections per day across the globe exceeded 8.3 billon. The connected ecosystem and increasing reach of Internet-of-Thing (IoT) enabled devices to facilitate consumer to pay from diversified geo-graphic locations and currencies. Half of the digital business transactions declined due to suspected fraud.

Three domain server protocol prevents fraudulent activities in card-based payment transactions through multiple channels and devices. It is widely adapted and utilized to secure the payment. The specification of advancement in 3DS2 is already formulated and available by Europay, MasterCard, Visa Contactless (EMVCo) [5]. Many organiza-tions have already started offering the 3DS2 services and capabilities to the connected ecosystems of payment. 3DS2 uses token-based and biometric authentication. It uses risk-based decisions for authentication using additional data during the transactions. The consumer checkout experience is anticipated to be seamless and secures irrespective of the devices, applications, and methods payment. The challenge for 3DS2 is the accuracy in identifying the risk factors and computing the risks in real-time. Due to the increased number of options introduced for real-time payment transactions, the evolution in risk factors, assessment, and corresponding computations are imminent.

Blockchain can modernize a payment and capture the evolving risks in real-time. It offers tokenization and authenticity of transactions between multiple parties with minimal operational and technical frictions [6]. However, Blockchain protocols and governance are immature to content the compliances associated with the eCommerce payments. Its ability to support the challenging non-functional requirements of payment services has yet to be proven [7]. We identified the Blockchain driven 3DS2 Service Fabric Architecture framework (BC2SF) formulation 3DS2 Application Programming Interfaces (APIs). The APIs can be classified and governed based on evolving char-acteristics of payment ecosystems. Additionally, the BC2SF supports the new way of digital payments introduced in the future by means of evolving digital technologies and payment industry including digital currencies.

The core component of the BC2SF is 3D Secure 2.0 Service Fabric (3DS2SF). The 3DS2 specification emphasizes on the real-time evaluation of modeling and analyzing the risk factors associated with the payment transactions. The BC provides detail history of the transaction in context of the digital payment to identify the risk factors and their rela-tionships with the ongoing transaction(s). The risks factors can have multiple or nested levels of dimensions. The examples of the dimensions for risk factors includes geoloca-tion, devices, applications, currency (or amount), internet connectivity paradigms, and products (or services). For instance, if the payment has been initiated from the unautho-rized or unrecognized device over the previous transactions pertaining to the related BC transactions of the specific person or eCommerce website then it requires computing risk on the specific digital payment transaction to identify the amount can be allowed for purchasing.

We investigated issues and challenges of digital payment due to advancements in digitalization of business and introduction of 3DS2 in existing payment ecosystem in Sect. 2. Section 3 outlines the requirements of 3DS2 and indictive coordination alongside Blockchain technology. Section 4 presents the BC2SF framework components and their responsibilities. It provides methodology to specify and evaluate risk factors to identify real-time authentication decision for payment ecosystem. Section 5 illustrates the empirical use case of charitable contribution during point-of-sale (PoS) using BC2SF. Eventually, Sect. 6 concludes our findings and future direction to advance the risk governance.

2   Challenges of Digital Payment Methods and 3DS2

Three Domain Secure (3DS) specification is primarily composed of acquirer domain, interoperability domain, and issuer domain, as indicated in Fig. 1. Acquirer establishes a relationship with a merchant to accept payment card transactions [8]. The acquirer domain has a requester client, server environment, integrator, and payment authorization mechanisms. The client can either be application-based or browser-based. The server collects necessary data elements for 3DS messages [5]. It authenticates, validates, and ensures the messages between the requester of the payment and cardholders.

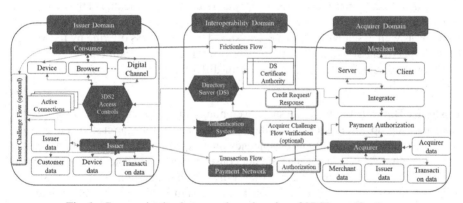

Fig. 1. Communication between three domains of 3DS2 specification.

The integrator provides the functional interface between the 3DS requestor environment and the 3D secure messages between client and server. The interoperability domain consists of Directory Server (DS), Directory Server Certificate Authority (DSCA), and Authorization System. The issuer domain manifests cardholder, consumer device, issuer information, and access control server (ACS).

3DS2 defines three types of client and server flows for the checkout process during any purchase irrespective of the digital payment channel or method, that is, frictionless flow, challenge flow, and transaction flow. Frictionless flow is new to 3DS2. Challenge flow and traditional transaction flow are associated and updated with frictionless flow requirements [8]. Frictionless flow [9] introduces risk-based authentication to determine whether the cardholder is required to perform challenge flow for further authentication. The risk-based authentication primarily dependents upon two factors, that is, the additional data captured during the checkout process of purchases and transaction history of the customer performing the payment. The data can be of multiple types, including cardholder purchasing behavioral pattern data, device information, and merchant authorization detail. Merchants are required to capture an extensive data set from the customer during the checkout process. The transaction flow retrieves the browser and mobile devices' data.

During our analysis of various approaches to implement 3DS2, we identified complexities and extendibility challenges of implying novel 3DS2 between client, acquirer, and interoperability domains. Following are the list of identified issues for 3DS2 to be effective.

Risk Factors: The risk factors vary for different types of businesses, geolocation, and personal profile of the individual. The 3DS2 needs to include dynamic of defining and configuring the risk factors depending on the different dimensions in consideration [10] and [11]. For instance, a customer with an international travel history and travel incentive account has a higher risk of currency level fraud and mishaps over online purchasing activities.

Payment Methodologies: The Internet-of-Thing (IoT) enabled devices advancing to capture new types of data to increase security and safeguard the identity of the individual. Client domains require to extend capabilities that can accept additional types of payment methods as well as authentication mechanisms. The MasterPass offering by the Master Card Corp. is a classic example of the new payment types [12]. Additionally, every bank and providers started offering the number of different ways to pay online as well as in-store purchases.

Customer Data: If the bank doesn't have enough information, then it can request a challenge step-up flow to authenticate the transaction and prompt the customer to provide additional data during 3DS2 The dependency on the quality of the data of the customers are very high. If the customer data are not consistent and up to date, then probabilities of the customers receiving the correct level of challenge question are lower [13]. The acquirers receive customer information from the card-issuing bank, public network, and government records during the card application. The data to verify the customer are typically old or not valid during the step-up flow to authenticate the transaction. Customer may have lived in the county for 3 to 4 weeks and may not have remembered it. Contrarily, an old acquittance, can take advantage of this information.

Payment Gateway Types: Generally, merchants facilitating eCommerce technologies utilize the payment gateway. The payment gateway providers implement the different encryption mechanisms as well as approval workflow for the transactions [14]. Any change or upgrade to the payment gateway requires either new interfaces or modification to the existing interfaces. Besides, the testing of the new or updated payment gateway with 3DS2 requires extensive testing before offering to the customers. Many types of payment gateways are available, including pro-hosted payment gateway and direct payment gateway. Pro-hosted payment gateway relies on the user data provided from the web or mobile application, whereas direct payment gateway periodically inquires the payment completion. Both the methods are for different purposes, and various types of messages flow between the merchant and payment gateway.

Merchant: 3DS2 emphasized on the authenticating the customers to avoid the fraudulent transaction. It has very little to no attention provided for malicious merchants and the validity of the merchant-specific device applications to accept the payment [15]. 3DS2 leverages the concept of the trusted merchant within the merchant account or the corresponding mobile applications. However, it is susceptible to exfiltrate. If the customer unknowingly configure browser to add trusted sites (as an add-on), then the third-party application during browsing can add the trusted merchant to the browser.

3 Synergy of 3DS2 Requirements and Blockchain Technologies

Internally, the 3DS2 server collects the necessary data elements from any or all the components to initiate the authentication. It has three types of information collected to analyze, that is, device information, browser information, and merchant risk information [5]. If a merchant has a mobile application with integration domain component of 3DS2, then it needs to capture the necessary information directly from the device to process the transaction. The device information consists of 12 data elements [16]. However, iOS-specific information has 13 elements, whereas Android-specific information has 36 elements. It includes the type of platform and the specific Internet Protocol (IP) address associated along with device name, device model, device's operating system information, time zone, location, and screen resolution. If transactions are conducted on the merchant's website through a browser, data is captured by the 3DS server. The browser information includes the content type, IP address, Java enablement flag, screen resolution, language, time zone, and user agent [5] information. The merchant is also required to collect additional cardholder information to help improve the accuracy of the risk-based authentication. The merchant risk information consists of account, purchase, prior transaction authentication, and account authentication information.

The merchant shares this information with the card issuer for analyses and identification of the risk level based on the specifics of the transaction. It allows the issuer to make an informed decision as to whether additional authentication step-up flow is required. The 3DS2 specification indicates computing the risk. If the risk is below a certain threshold, then the issuer will approve the cardholder authentication. For this specification to handle the transaction, it must generate Payment Tokens (PTs) for risk-based authentication. The PTs ranges are shared and configured on the DS. PTs routed to the DS and consequently to the ACS. During the transaction, the authentication request needs to detokenize PTs. The PT Indicator in the request message provides the risk associated with the transaction.

In [17], an extensive fraud processing method provides a merchant to implement discounting, acceptance, and fraud rules based on the card type. It emphasizes on the risk with the card types over the risk levels associated with the consumers and the patterns of transactions. On the other hand, the method identified in [18] focuses on authentication system. It computes the decision based on device data during a checkout process of a current transaction on a merchant website and contextual data of the customer. The risk scoring mechanism for payment card transaction presented in [19] is based at least in part on the transaction data and infrastructure data associated with the transaction. It defines the acceptable risk to the merchant against the pre-defined risk threshold. Data mining techniques including decision tree, logistic regression, random forest and neural network were constructed with the cleaned dataset to detect risks of credit card defaulters in [20]. It predicts risk associated with merchants with credit card defaulters with 82% accuracy. The comparative analysis is presented in [21] with multiple machine learning (ML) classification on the highly imbalanced datasets consisting of credit card transactions. It indicates that any additional datasets linked with consumers to be considered to identify risks and changing the threshold require merchants to undertake a hefty level of assumptions in their risk classification. The existing approaches are incompetent to evolve the merchant's payment ecosystem in a way to insert or update the risk levels as well as new paradigms to compute the risks at runtime during transaction processing.

A blockchain consists of a peer-to-peer (P2P) communication overlay network. Each network node connects to other nodes through defined protocol and discovery processes [22]. The research presented in [23] takes advantage of the delay-tolerant nature of blockchains to deliver banking services to remote communities. The blockchain users can handle regular transaction processing with the use of a base station feature capabilities offering connectivity within the local area. The bank only joins in processing currency exchange requests. In [24], the conceptual architecture for a blockchain-based Personal Data and Identity Management System (BPDIMS) is illustrated using trust protocol and off-chain repository.

The decentralized and distributed linked list built with hash pointers [25] is available to all participants involved in the payment transactions in Blockchain-based payment authentication. [26] establishes a new architecture called secure pub-sub (SPS) without middleware, that is, blockchain-based fair payment with reputation. In SPS, publishers publish a topic on the blockchain, and subscribers specify a message by depositing to the topic. The [27] prescribes Blockchain digital certificate methodology to avoid fraudulent transactions. It generates a digital certificate for the transaction data by blockchain-enabled electronic ownership token. It allows transferring the electronic ownership of the token.

The blockchain-enabled ecosystem can provide the following advantages and resolves challenges of 3DS2 specification to be implemented for the payment networks.

- Blockchain protocol consistently connects and communicate customers, merchant, acquirer, issuers, and payment, gateway providers. It can provision role-based transaction information in the nodes.
- The block maintains the chain of transactions and associated risks for a specific customer (or set of customers). It achieves the prior transaction authentication requirements of 3DS2 without real-time computation as a recent transaction block already carries the authentication information with it.

- Blockchain allows customization of tokens in consideration of many dimensions and risk factors including device, browser, and merchant information specified by 3DS2. It can validate merchant and cardholders (customers) in the specification of the token.
- The blocks can be extended as well as interoperable with the new transactional and IoT device information. It can also include these factors for risk computation and authentication.

The blockchain configuration includes consensus in the perception of validator nodes for the issuer to validate blocks with the transactions [28]. Consequently, different types of consensus can be implied depending on the type of participant in the transaction, that is, public, private, and permissioned (or consortium) blockchain. Typically, 3DS2 is a candidate of consortium blockchain where participants are pre-selected, and the issuer has the authorization to modify the participant list.

4   Blockchain Driven 3DS2 Service Fabric Architecture Framework

To address and resolve the challenges of managing complexities of PTs of 3DS2 in the conditions of computing risks in real-time, we have identified the Blockchain driven 3DS2 Service Fabric Architecture (BC2SF). It correlates, computes, and advances risks associated with the specific transaction under the influence of changing characteristics of risks factors through Blockchain-enabled services or Application Programming Interfaces (APIs). The blockchain nodes include a trace or period trace of the transaction history beginning at the activation of the cards to the most recent payment in terms of blocks. It inherits detail of the transactions for each consumer, including device, browser, and merchant risk information required by 3DS2 specification. The transactions in the blocks are not limited to a specific card; it has the link to the potential payments associated with the consumers whether it is performed utilizing any device, card, or other means of payment. The services under the Blockchain network provision shared repositories and common processes in the nodes to compute the risks based on the risk factors in the context of the transaction. It entails an efficient and accurate specification of risks associated with payments.

Figure 2 provides components of the BC2SF incorporating friction fewer payment options and real-time risk computing capabilities. The primary components of the BC2SF framework are 3DS2 service fabric (3DS2Sf), Blockchain API Manager (BCAPIm), Authentication Decision Manager (ADm), Blockchain Node Manager (BNm), Acquirer Configurator (Acon), and Digital Channel Director (DCd). 3DS2Sf is formulated with Risk Factor Association Manager (RFAm), Risk Rater (RRt), Risk Orchestrator (ROr), and Risk Feedback Engine (RFe).

3DS2 Service Fabric (3DS2Sf): The primary responsibility of the 3DS2Sf is to provide the platform to integrate the acquirer domain, interoperability domain, and issuer domain through the services (or APIs). The 3DS2Sf invokes the frictionless flow of the 3DS2 specification through service. It evaluates the risks associated with the transactions based on the risk factors and risk rating techniques utilized for the specific classification of the service for the type of transaction chain maintained within the Blockchain network nodes. It is accountable to decide whether the transaction needs one more level of further

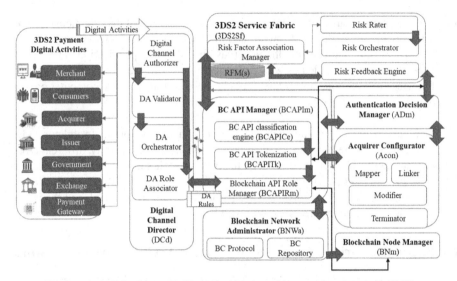

Fig. 2. Blockchain driven 3DS2 service fabric architecture framework (BC2SF).

authentication. 3DS2Sf connects with the ADm with analyzed information within the services for further action towards the payment transaction in context.

Risk Factor Association Manager (RFAm): RFAm defines RFA (Risk Factor Association) model (RFM) to identify, place, and compute risk factors associated with the specific transaction or set of transactions in real-time. RFM consists of risks factors for the device, browsers, and merchant risk authentication. It can also consist of subcategories of risk factors for each of the data elements associated with the device, browser, and merchant risk authentication during the payment. Figure 3 represents the elements of the RFM. RFM provides the contract and agreement between the issuers, merchants, acquirers, and cardholders in adherence to avoid fraudulent digital activities during frictionless flow for payment. In Fig. 3, RIC represents the risk computations, "n" presents the number of participants' digital activities, and "r" characterizes number of risks for the particular digital activity in context.

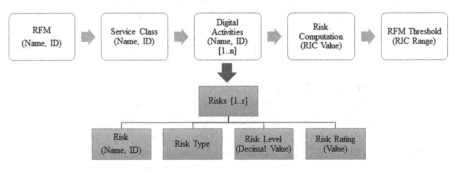

Fig. 3. Risk factor association model (RFM) elements.

Risk Rater (RRt): RRt is to define the type of risk and its rating when it occurs during the transaction flow within the 3DS2 ecosystem. The risk rating scheme can be changed in real-time through RRt component of the RFAm. The real-time change in the RRt scheme (or technique) will be implied either to the specific types or set of transactions in the proximity of the RFA model.

Risk Orchestrator (ROr): ROr provides the hierarchy of the risks across the RFM. The ROr specifies the order of risks from high to low. The RFM can either define, adapt, or dynamically change risk orchestration using ROr. The ROr dilutes the rating of the specific risk in real-time by the delta specified within the RFM depending on the position of the risk in the orchestration.

Risk Feedback Engine (RFe): RFe is the sanity check whether the computed risks are within the range of specific threshold. It specifies and adjusts the risk threshold for RFA model. If the transaction is supposed to be unauthorized, however, it is computed to be authorized, then it decreases the threshold for future transactions of the same type corresponding to the associated risk factors.

Authentication Decision Manager (ADm): ADm is the final decision provided whether the frictionless flow must go through additional authorization, denied, or approved. It validates the computation performed using RFAm and the risk threshold from the RFe to provide the decision for each transaction. The runtime validation of risk threshold for a specific type of transaction can only be performed using ADm. ADm interacts with BCAPIm and BNm to initiate either challenge flow or transaction flow required to proceed with the purchase or transaction. ADm is also the final authority to decide on challenge flow upon receiving additional information of the cardholder. It identifies the cardholder and authorized to proceed with the transaction or disapprove the transaction. It again informs BCAPIm to initiate transaction flow.

Blockchain API Manager (BCAPIm): BCAPIm is responsible for classification, management, and error handling of services. Each RFM is mapped to the service (or API) to compute the risks associated with the payment transaction(s). The challenge flow and transaction flow are also associated with the specific APIs within the BCAPIm. If the ADm doesn't approve the frictionless flow and it needs to initiate the challenge flow API, then BCAPIm initiates the challenge flow to receive more information from the cardholder. It connects with ADm to take further action against the information received. If the transaction flow is initiated by ADm, then BCAPIm's transaction flow APIs performs the transaction and registers it to the block associated with the Blockchain node through BNm.

BC API classification engine (BCAPICe), Blockchain API Role Manager (BCAPIRm), and BC API Tokenization (BCAPITk) are the essential components of the BCAPIm. BCAPICe specifies the classification of the services interacting with BC nodes and frictionless payment. Acquirer associated with the merchant (or set of merchants) can define the classification scheme. It can be based on the type of transaction, geolocation diversity, type of merchants, type of devices, mobile applications, type of consumers, and other customarily defined class. The acquirer can select to place classification with multiple dimensions.

BCAPITk connects BCAPICe and 3DS2Sf to recognize RFM for the specific classification through ADm. It identifies the RFM to be implied for the specific transaction based on the classification specified by the acquirer. It provides access and visibility of the transaction chains associated with the specific transaction with the token and its accessibility for the merchant and issuing bank. The ADm executes the specified RFM and computes the risks in real-time. The BCAPITk generates the token and associate computed risk to it.

BCAPIRm provides the accessibility of the token to various participants of the transaction. The transaction may involve multiple issuers, merchants, brokers, cardholders, and acquirers. Each participant can have a specific role. BCAPIRm manages the role hierarchy and rules associated with the roles during the transaction. BCAPIRm also defines the validator role responsible for validating the Blockchain nodes.

Blockchain Node Manager (BNm): The transfer of information between Blockchain and BCAPIm in the framework occurs using a cryptographic protocol that arrives at a consensus among participant nodes to update the blocks. BNm defines the consensus mechanism based on the Blockchain topologies selected within the payment ecosystem, that is, private, public, or permissioned (or consortium) blockchain. The BNm in association with the BCAPIRm manages the accessibility of the Blockchain nodes and their blocks. It also performs validation of the nodes recognizing validator assigned by the BCAPIRm.

Blockchain Network Administrator (BNWa): The BNWa provides administrative aspects of Blockchain to connect acquirers, merchants, issuers, and consumers in the vicinity of the transactions through the Blockchain nodes. Multiple blockchain protocols can be utilized to achieve consensus among participant nodes for updating the blockchain ledger. Each such protocol will have to be evaluated in the context of the participants of payment and transaction, the use case, and requirements of an enterprise. If the payment gateway is utilized intermediator, then it can either introduce or leverage one or more protocols to recognize and validate the transaction. BNWa provides capabilities to establish the protocol and streamline communication between the BCAPIm and blocks of shared repository carrying the history associated with the specific transaction in context.

Acquirer Configurator (Acon): The Acon is responsible for administering each service under the scope of specific acquirer or type of acquirer. It is composed of four different elements of service administration, that is, Mapper, Linker, Modifier, and Terminator. It interfaces with BCAPIm and 3DS2Sf to map the services (or APIs) the frictionless, challenge, and transaction flows. The Acon linker establishes links between the RFM and APIs. The Acon modifier updates the mapping and linking at runtime. It also maintains the versions of the updated mapping and linking. Acon terminator is accountable for successfully dismiss the invalid and unauthorized transactions as recommended by the ADm. The terminated transaction is also recorded to the blockchain node through BCAPIm.

Digital Channel Director (DCd): The DCd provides the means to connect diversified users with the BC2SF framework. The customer, issuer, merchant, and acquirer can utilize many ways to perform various activities during the checkout process of the purchases, as indicated in the responsibilities of each component. DCd is responsible for validating and orchestrating these activities. It is also the first line of defense against faulty payment activities and transactions. It consists of Digital Channel Authorizer (DCa), Digital Activity Validator (DAv), Digital Activity Orchestrator (DAo), and Digital Channel Role Associator (DCr). DCa authorizes new or existing digital channel for the payment. DAv validates the activities and Dao orchestrator the digital activities in alignment with the checkout process, including receiving payment information and biometrics of the cardholder. DCr associate the role of the specific digital activity with the BCAPIRm to recognize the rules to be implied for the specific digital activity.

The digital activities, the roles associated with digital activities, and actions differ significantly across the checkout process. It is eminent during in-store purchases as well. For example, the cardholder decides to pay with the mobile payment application for the groceries as well as the eye examination performed in the supermarket, facilitating both the capabilities. Multiple merchants, banks, and insurance company participate during the transaction. The risk factors with the transaction need to be analyzed at runtime as multiple types of payments are included in the transaction. The RFAm associates the risk factors, the orchestration of risks, and individual risk rating in the unified RFM as API. The risk can be computed for the entire transaction (in Block Ia). The ADm registers the transaction to block as authorized transaction upon approval. The Blockchain has capabilities to link the transaction through blocks for merchants as well as cardholders. For instance, if the cardholder has a secondary card issued to the family member, then ADm immediately links and compute the risks corresponding to the inflight transaction (in Block Ib) by the secondary card. If one of the identified risk factors is the payment limit with the threshold of the $250, then ADm ensures the accumulative payment for both transactions (Block Ia and Block Ib). If the amount exceeds the $250 threshold, then it rejects the later transaction (Block Ib). However, the rejected transaction (Block Ib) still been recorded for future reference to compute the risk for the subsequent transaction (in Block II).

BC2SF enables to build an industry-agnostic payment ecosystem to complete the implementation of 3DS2 specification within the dilemma increasing number of digital channels for payment. It prohibits fraudulent digital activities and provides early indicators equally to the cardholder and merchants. It brings role-based transparency and accuracy between acquirers and issuers. 3DS2Sf and ADm recognizes and ensures the existing, new, and updated risks of digital activities during the checkout process and payment transactions. The BC2SF also resolves interoperability challenges and transparency between participants of the payment ecosystem to recognize the risks with the transactions.

5   In-store and Online Charitable Contribution Use Case of BC2SF

Charitable Giving Report indicates that the most common approach preferred by the consumers for charitable donation over two years was checkout donations during point-of-sale (PoS) purchases [26]. 2018 survey reveals that 79 charitable contribution campaign initiatives brought in $486.37 million [24]. Charitable contribution campaigns are crucial for not-for-profit or nonprofits to achieve the target for noble causes. Individual giving makes up nearly 70% of donations around the globe [29]. According to the National Center for Charitable Statistics, 1.56 million tax-exempt organizations exist in the United States [30]. The organizations must enable digital channels in compelling ways to donate and contribute to charity events. Blackbaud's 2017 Charitable Giving Report indicates that the most common approach preferred by the consumers for charitable donation over two years was checkout donations during point-of-sale (PoS) purchases [31]. 2018 survey reveals that 79 charitable contribution campaign initiatives brought in $486.37 million [29].

As retailers increase their digital presence and work to offer 3DS2 frictionless payment options to their consumers, they are also bringing nonprofit counterparts along with the point-of-sale systems [29]. It raises a need for a system that allows the consumer to donate to charitable trust or organization based on having observed them [32]. It is useful for the consumer to be able to restrict how the recipient spent donation through selecting charitable trust or a specific campaign. It is mandatory to secure delivery of the donation to the recipient to prevent fraudulent recipients. A merchant's PoS terminals and online checkouts can prompt micro-donations for local and national nonprofits and adding a donation to a specific charity campaign. The BC2SF can seamlessly handle the scenario and dynamically update the list of nonprofits, not-for-profit, or charitable contribution campaigns as a workflow. We identified 15 metalevel activities requires to be performed during the checkout of purchases to accommodate charitable contribution. Table 1 represents the RFM associated with service classification "Member Donation". The RFM provides the example risk rating (RR), risk level (RL), DA Threshold (DAT), and RFM threshold (T) to define the relationship between the merchant, consumer, and charitable trust. T provides the acceptable range to approve the transaction for purchases and donation.

All the branches of the merchant or set of merchants associated with acquirer utilizing BC2SF can have consistent RFM across their value-chain. The RFM can also have diversification based on various dimensions in the Blockchain network. For instance, if the RFM focused on the United States, then the service class needs to be "United State Member Donation" through BCAPICe. Although each merchant can generate its way to compute the overall risk associated with RFM and risk rating scheme for the RFM, we created risk computation (RIC) based on Eq. 1.

$$\text{RIC} = \left(\sum_{i=1}^{n} (RLi X RRi) \right) \Big/ \text{n} \qquad (1)$$

"n" presents the total number of DA for the specific service classification. The RR represents the risk rating between 1 to 5 where DA with risk rating 1 is at the lowest risk and 5 is at the highest risk provided by the RRt. The RL specifies the risk level in the orchestration of the risk retrieved from the ROr. The RIC considers the averaging the product of risk level and risk rating associated with each digital activity. The formula indicates the precedence of the risks associated with the lower-level digital activities in the hierarchy is 10% higher than the previous level of digital activities. For example, DA# 1, DA# 2, and DA# 5 are at the risk level 1 and RL is 1 for them in Table 1. DA# 3 (underneath DA# 2) and DA# 6 (underneath DA# 5) are at risk level 2 and RL is 1.1 for them. DA# 13 and DA# 14 are at nested level of DA# 12 as the digital activities

Table 1. Digital activities of member donation service.

RFM: POS charitable contribution
Service classification: member donation

DA#	DA	Role	Risk	RL	RR	DAT
1	Enter purchase amount	Merchant	Items or number of purchased items	Level 1a	1	
2	Enter card number	Consumer	Customer privacy	Level 1b	5	≪4-digit range≫
3	Enter donation amount (with purchase)	Consumer	In appropriate donation amount	Level 1b.1	2	10% (of purchases)
4	Select & validate charitable trust	Consumer	Classification & rating of charitable trust	Level 1b.2	3	
5	Receive & validate card holder	Acquirer	Invalid person or transaction	Level 1c	2	
6	Verify purchase and donation amount based on card transactions	Payment gateway (or acquirer)	In appropriate amount or exceeding threshold value	Level 1c.1	2	$250
7	Approve & notify card holder	Acquirer	No activities & invalid transaction history	Level 1c.2	4	
8	Challenge questions (if required)	Acquirer	Invalid challenge questions & answers	Level 1c.3	3	≪Pre-authorized questions≫
9	Pay & deduct amount from card holder for purchase	Issuer	Card holder credentials & amount	Level 1d	2	
10	Receive amount for purchases	Merchant	Account not available for deposit	Level 1d.1	2	

(continued)

Table 1. (*continued*)

RFM: POS charitable contribution
Service classification: member donation

DA#	DA	Role	Risk	RL	RR	DAT
11	Pay & deduct amount for donation	Issuer	Card holder credentials & amount	Level 1e	3	
12	Receive donation amount	Charitable trust	Account not available for deposit	Level 1e.1	2	
13	Tax deduction & exemption	Charitable trust	Mismatching of Tax codes & amount	Level 1e.11	2	≪Tax codes for charity≫
14	Tax authorization & notification	Charitable trust	Unauthorized category of donation	Level 1e.12	3	≪Donation categories≫
15	Tax computation & credits	Government	Unregistered tax information & codes	Level 1f	2	≪Tax exempt organizations≫

RIC = 2.78. **T** (for transaction to be approved) = [0 to 3]

are performed by the charitable trust in association to the government irrespective of the consumer or type of consumer. It is the reason, the RL is 1.11 for DA# 13 and 1.12 for DA# 14 indicating the risk is only 1% incrementally higher over the primary digital activity, that is, DA# 12.

The BC enables token to carry the RFM with its RIC. BCAPITk manages all the issued tokens across BC network. The value of the token is consistent between all the participants, including merchant, acquirer, issuer, charitable trust, and government. The ADm decides based on the runtime value of the RIC against the threshold defined for RFM to approve the transaction. ADm can facilitate the transaction for purchases, however, rejecting the donation amount through the Acon modifier using the API dedicated to the charitable contribution campaign event defined in BCAPIm. The BNm ensures to register the transaction irrespective of the approved or rejected by ADm. It is utilized by acquirer during the subsequent transaction by the consumer at the same or different merchant to identify RR for the DA, as indicated in Table 1. DA# 7. Based on the status of the transaction, the RFe provides feedback to RFAm and adjust the RR for the specific risk associated with DA through RRt component.

The BC2SF heavily relies on APIs to process and validate transactions as well as to insert the risk levels and thresholds. BCAPIm is responsible to discover APIs in correlation to transaction and risk in real-time. The BCAPIm quality-of-service (QoS) across the payment ecosystem improves the discovery of the APIs at runtime as indicated in [33]. The challenge for the acquirer is to select the appropriate QoS model based on the learnings of the number of transactions of a specific pattern and the type of consumers. The acquirer will not have visibility of all the transactions performed by the specific type of consumers as consumers utilize diversified payment methods issued by different banks. The acquirer needs to adapt QoS prediction model [34] to improve the prediction accuracy between the APIs to compute and insert risk levels at runtime. 3DS2Sf's API consumptions require to be based on the recognized combination of historic and predicated transaction patterns.

The advancements in 3DS2 require many organizations to include different scenarios and diversification in the payment transactions during purchases. In [35], the extensible PoS device is identified to register a third-party application for changing transaction on the PoS device for merchants. It provides a user interface during a purchase using one of a registered application module and a payment module. [36] claims that the charity collection processes are not transparent and charitable organizations struggle to gain donors' trust and interest. The proposed blockchain-based charity management platform provides a seamless, secure, auditable, and efficient system. It enables charity collection process using crypto wallets, Initial Coin Offering (ICO), economic model, and introduces CharityCoin (CC) as a digital currency.

6   Conclusion

In this paper, we presented the blockchain services-based framework to implement 3DS2. The primary differentiation to implement 3DS2 is the runtime risk computing for the transaction during the payment. The BC2SF architecture framework provides APIs to capture and utilize device data, browser (or mobile application) data, merchant risk data to compute risks and embed the RIC with tokens in real-time for each transaction. Blockchain enables the granular level of risks accuracy based on the DA and associated roles. It decreases the complexity and difficulty of analyzing transaction history during the purchases and correlate them with the risk of the new transaction. The tokenization and RIC scheme of BC2SF introduces risk computation capabilities for all the participants in the transaction, including the consumers, merchant, acquirers, and issuers. BCAPIm implements core functions of frictionless payment and challenge flow specified in3DS2 standards. It is extensible to update and generate service classifications based on the dimensions and in advancements of digital channels. BC2SF DCd seamlessly integrates upcoming methods of payments to facilitate consumers and merchants, including digital wallet capabilities.

BC2SF promotes configurable solution for the payment methods with real-time decisions on authentication and non-payment user authentication. It dynamically extends services to meet specific regulatory requirements, including proprietary out-of-band authentication solutions by card issuers. The benefits are visible for 3DS2 risk-based authentication, tokenization, and evolving paradigms for risk assessment during frictionless payment utilizing BC2SF. The primary research interest is to advance BC2SF governance processes considering different types of business transactions and automation among participants of the payment ecosystem.

References

1. Guta, M.: 27% of Online Sales End Up Being Fraudulent Transactions, Small Business Trends, December 2019
2. Federal Reserve Bank of Minneapolis: Fighting Fraud in the e-Commerce Channel: A Merchant Study, June 2018
3. The Nilson Report, Card Fraud Losses Reach $27.85 Billion, November 2019
4. Liu, S.: Internet of Things - Statistics & Facts, Statista, March 2020
5. EMVCo, LLC: EMV 3-D Secure Protocol and Core Functions Specification v2.2.0, December 2018
6. Wu, A., Zhang, Y., Zheng, X., Guo, R., Zhao, Q., Zheng, D.: Efficient and privacy-preserving traceable attribute-based encryption in blockchain. Ann. Telecommun. **74**(7–8), 401–411 (2019)
7. Hasan, H.R., Salah, K.: Proof of delivery of digital assets using blockchain and smart contracts. IEEE Access **6**, 65439–65448 (2018)
8. Corella, F., Lewison, K.P.: Frictionless web payments with cryptographic cardholder authentication. In: Stephanidis, C. (ed.) HCII 2019. LNCS, vol. 11786, pp. 468–483. Springer, Cham (2019). https://doi.org/10.1007/978-3-030-30033-3_36
9. Corella, F., Lewison, K.P., Pomian and Corella LLC: Scheme for frictionless cardholder authentication. U.S. Patent Application 16/533,771 (2020)
10. Ab Hamid, N.R., Cheng, A.Y.: A risk perception analysis on the use of electronic payment systems by young adult. order **6**(8.4), 6–7 (2020)
11. Ali, M.A., van Moorsel, A.: Designed to be broken: a reverse engineering study of the 3D secure 2.0 payment protocol. In: Goldberg, I., Moore, T. (eds.) FC 2019. LNCS, vol. 11598, pp. 201–221. Springer, Cham (2019). https://doi.org/10.1007/978-3-030-32101-7_13
12. Shrilatha, S., Priya, M.M.L.: The role of customers to attain sustainable development of cashless transaction by shifting to mobile wallets at Vellore city. Stud. Indian Place Names **40**(18), 11–29 (2020)
13. Ma, S., Fildes, R.: Forecasting third-party mobile payments with implications for customer flow prediction. Int. J. Forecast. **36**(3), 739–760 (2020)
14. Dhobe, S.D., Tighare, K.K., Dake, S.S.: A review on prevention of fraud in electronic payment gateway using secret code. Int. J. Res. Eng. Sci. Manag. **3**(1), 602–606 (2020)
15. Corella, F., Lewison, K.: Fundamental Security Flaws in the 3-D Secure 2 Cardholder Authentication Specification (2019)
16. EMVCo, LLC: EMV 3-D Secure SDK—Device Information Data Version 1.4, October 2019
17. Weber, L.: Account type detection for fraud risk, Visa International Service Association, United States patent application US 16/367,935 (2019)
18. Tomasofsky, C.P., et al.: Systems and methods for providing risk based decisioning service to a merchant, Mastercard International Inc., United States patent US 10,614,452 (2020)
19. Roche, M.F., Salaman, K.: Decision making on-line transactions, US Bancorp, National Association, United States patent application US 16/164,609 (2020)
20. Leong, O.J., Jayabalan, M.: A comparative study on credit card default risk predictive model. J. Comput. Theor. Nanosci. **16**(8), 3591–3595 (2019)
21. Parthasarathy, G., et al.: Comparative Case Study of Machine Learning Classification Techniques Using Imbalanced Credit Card Fraud Datasets, SSRN 3351584 (2019)
22. Xia, Q., Sifah, E.B., Huang, K., Chen, R., Du, X., Gao, J.: Secure payment routing protocol for economic systems based on blockchain. In: 2018 International Conference on Computing, Networking and Communications (ICNC), pp. 177–181. IEEE, March 2018
23. Hu, Y., et al.: A delay-tolerant payment scheme based on the ethereum blockchain. IEEE Access **7**, 33159–33172 (2019)

24. Faber, B., Michelet, G.C., Weidmann, N., Mukkamala, R.R., Vatrapu, R.: BPDIMS: a blockchain-based personal data and identity management system. In: Proceedings of the 52nd Hawaii International Conference on System Sciences, January 2019
25. Godfrey-Welch, D., Lagrois, R., Law, J., Anderwald, R.S.: Blockchain in payment card systems. SMU Data Sci. Rev. **1**(1), 3 (2018)
26. Zhao, Y., Li, Y., Mu, Q., Yang, B., Yu, Y.: Secure pub-sub: blockchain-based fair payment with reputation for reliable cyber physical systems. IEEE Access **6**, 12295–12303 (2018)
27. Allen, C.M., Hale, C., Nomura, C.: Systems and Methods that Utilize Blockchain Digital Certificates for Data Transactions, Kountable Inc., U.S. Patent Application 15/787,674 (2018)
28. Zouina, M., Outtai, B.: Towards a distributed token-based payment system using blockchain technology. In: 2019 International Conference on Advanced Communication Technologies and Networking (CommNet), pp. 1–10. IEEE, April 2019
29. Hessekiel, D.: Charity Checkout Remains Strong, Even In A Changing Retail Landscape, Leadership Strategy, Forbes Media LLC (2020)
30. McKeever, B.: The Nonprofit Sector in Brief 2018, National Center for Charitable Statistics, December 2018
31. Blackbaud Institute: 2018 Charitable Giving Report: How Fundraising Performed in 2018, February 2019
32. Bax, N.G.: Identifying Recipients for Restricted Giving. U.S. Patent Application 16/045,681 (2020)
33. Sha, J., Du, Y., Qi, L.: A user requirement-oriented web service discovery approach based on logic and threshold petri net. IEEE/CAA J. Automatica Sinica **6**(6), 1528–1542 (2019)
34. Luo, X., et al.: Generating highly accurate predictions for missing QoS data via aggregating nonnegative latent factor models. IEEE Trans. Neural Netw. Learn. Syst. **27**(3), 524–537 (2015)
35. Beatty, J.D., El Calamawy, T.M., Abrams, J.W., Quinlan, M.J., Blattman, J.: Extensible point-of-sale platforms and associated methods, Clover Network Inc., U.S. Patent 10,580,029 (2020)
36. Farooq, M.S., Khan, M., Abid, A.: A framework to make charity collection transparent and auditable using blockchain technology. Comput. Electr. Eng. **83**, 106588 (2020)

Educational Application of Big Data Research: A Comparison of China and US

Ting Zhang[1]([⊠]) [iD], Clara Elizabeth[2], and Renzhi Cao[2] [iD]

[1] Beijing Jiaotong University, Beijing 100044, China
zhangt@plu.edu
[2] Pacific Lutheran University, Tacoma, WA 98447, USA
caora@plu.edu

Abstract. Huge amount of data is generated each day, and big data research can be applied in various fields to analyze and extract new knowledge from this big amount of data, with education being one of the most important applications. However, few researchers are focused on comparative analysis of big data application in education between China and the US. In this paper, we analyze the differences between these two countries in their applications of big data theory to the education field. In addition, we also discuss the ethical challenges of these applications, such as how China and US protect privacy in the educational field when applying big data research. Finally, this paper also discusses the lessons learned from the development of big data applications to the education field. This includes privacy protection, which could be used to help policy makers of countries around the world regulate the application of big data theory in the education field.

Keywords: Big data · Education · Application · Privacy

1 Introduction

The big data White Paper "Big Data for Development: Challenges & Opportunities," released by the United Nations in 2012, pointed out that "Big Data is a sea change that, like nanotechnology and quantum computing, will shape the twenty-first century" [1]. In recent years, with the development of cloud computing, big data and data intensive science, massive data has penetrated into all walks of life and has an important impact on social life.

Currently, the field of education is marked by the rise and application of information technology (especially big data technology) and the non-linear growth of education data driven by the data age. Due to this, big data is becoming a new driving force that cannot be ignored in the field of education. Complementing this, the application of educational data mining and learning analysis technology makes the hidden value of education data surface day by day. The U.S. Department of Education pointed out that mining and analysis of big data in education can promote the reform of the teaching system in American colleges, universities, and K-12 schools in October 2012 [2]. In August 2015, the State Council of China reported, "building big data in education and

© Springer Nature Switzerland AG 2020
J. E. Ferreira et al. (Eds.): SERVICES 2020, LNCS 12411, pp. 28–42, 2020.
https://doi.org/10.1007/978-3-030-59595-1_3

culture, exploring and supporting the role of big data in transforming education methods, promoting education equity, and improving education quality [3]." In May 2016, J Mervis in Science journal reported in support of big data, recommending "the development and evaluation of innovative learning opportunities and educational pathways" as future investments [4]. It is clear that big data in education has attracted widespread attention.

The International Data Center IDC described four significant characteristics of big data in 2011: volumes (size and/or rate), variety (structured and unstructured), velocity (real-time or near-real-time), and value (huge value, but low density) [5]. Big data in education is not only the application of big data technology in the field of education, but also an independent branch that drives the differentiation of big data technology through the education industry. In its definition, some researchers consider big data in education as a subset of big data, specifically referring to big data in the field of education, which is generated during the entire educational activity process and collected according to educational needs. It is used for educational development, and has great potential value [6].

There are several notable aspects of a definition for big data in education. The first is the aspect of composition. Big data in education comes from the subjects and processes of education and teaching. This includes individuals, schools, regions and Countries, including basic data, management data, teaching data, scientific research data, service data, and other types of multi-dimensional, multi-dimensional, diverse sources of huge data sets. The second aspect is the educational characteristic. The cycle of education determines the typical periodicity of big data in education. At the same time, the complexity of the education process makes the analysis of big data in education more difficult, which requires new data processing and analysis technology. The third aspect is that the development goal of big data in education is to improve education and teaching, and to develop education as a whole. In this sense, big data in education is not the only thing that highlights the amount of data as "big", but more importantly, it has a "big" effect.

Compared with traditional education data, big data in education has stronger real-time, periodicity and continuity. Compared with the traditional statistical analysis of education data, the analysis of big data in education is more complex and comprehensive. The combination of big data and education will also have an unprecedented impact on the development of education.

2   Application of Big Data in Education

From the perspective of needs, the application of big data in education can be summarized into four levels: teaching, management, evaluation and policy (see Fig. 1). The teaching layer focuses on adaptive teaching and learning; the management layer focuses on precise and scientific management and services; the evaluation layer focuses on discovering the laws of education and teaching; the policy layer focuses on the continuous improvement of education policies.

Big data in education can be used to improve teaching models and teaching quality. The traditional teaching model is mainly teachers based, and the teaching goal is mainly achieved by the teachers' explanation of knowledge. The application of big data in education technology can allow teachers to better understand the learning status of

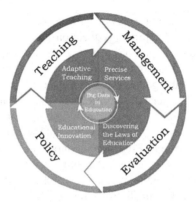

Fig. 1. Application of big data in education diagram.

students, and help teachers to adjust teaching plans and methods in a timely manner. For students, students' understanding of their own learning conditions will promote students to better understand themselves.

Big data in education is conducive to achieving scientific management and accurate services. The scope of traditional information acquisition in education is limited, making the overall level of education management low. Big data technology allows us to obtain and store massive data in a timely and fast manner. The quality of education could be highly improved. At the same time, the analysis of various "pain points" in management services, such as the analysis of early warning data for student management, can effectively provide school teachers and students with more refined and scientific services and improve the management level of education and teaching.

Traditional teaching evaluation forms are relatively simple, and most of them use qualitative evaluations. A large amount of real and reliable data can help us to get rid of "empiricism" in teaching evaluation and gradually move towards "Dadaism". Through the "induction" of a large amount of data, the laws of education and teaching activities are found. These laws will help educational subjects—students and teachers to reflect on teaching and learning, thereby promoting and optimizing educational and teaching activities.

The traditional form of educational decision-making in China is often referred to as "brain-head" decision-making. Policy makers often disregard the actual situation and formulate policies based on their own ideas, experience or speculation. With the advent of the era of big data in education, education will no longer be a social science that is inherited by ideas and experience. Through the analysis of education data, the teaching, learning, and evaluation are found to be in line with the actual situation of students and teaching. Technology could help to turn data into knowledge, so that education policies can be formulated in a targeted manner. This keeps education and teaching strategies more in line with reality in order to promote the reform and development of education and teaching.

3   Comparison of Big Data in Education Between China and US

See Table 1.

Table 1. Comparison of big data in education between China and the US

Category	China	US
Educational resources	High teacher-student ratio Solve the dilemma of student management and teaching	Low teacher-student ratio Adaptive learning and management
Education systems	System-managed student affairs management model Reduce or optimize the teaching and management work	Service-oriented management model Provide students with various types of learning help
Data collection	No standard process for the collection of data In-depth analysis of university data, lack of regional and national analysis	Relatively complete system for the collection of data More complete data at all levels
Significance	Data analysis results for reference Big data systems with few direct aids in decision making	Value the results of data analysis Formed many big data systems to assist decision-making

3.1   Differences in Educational Resources Between China and US Put Different Requirements on Big Data in Education

Although the student-teacher ratio of Chinese universities has basically reached or exceeded the standard of excellent student-teacher ratios set by the Chinese Ministry of Education (16: 1) [7], it is still far from the high-level universities in US. For example, the student-teacher ratio of Tsinghua University and Peking University in China is 13.99 (https://www.tsinghua.edu.cn/publish/newthu/newthu_cnt/about/about-6.html) and 13.32 (https://xxgk.pku.edu.cn/docs/20191009100710222522.pdf), but universities in US like Yale University, have a student-teacher ratio of approximately 6.27 (https://www.yale.edu/about-yale/yale-facts).

A reasonable student-teacher ratio could help students through interactions, and big data could help us to better understand learning rules through quantified learning behavior, make accurate predictions and implement teaching interventions. For example, the Massive Open Online Courses (MOOCs) has been widely adopted in US. Through the collection of massive educational data and the quantification of learning behaviors, it helps to deepen the knowledge of education rules and improve quality and efficiency of learning [8]. The "Degree Compass" personalized course recommendation system adopted by Austin Peay State University is a successful case of personalized education based on learning analysis [9]. Georgia State University, based on the data of previous graduates, identified specific high school students who may have difficulty connecting with university studies to provide summer tuition opportunities, which is also a typical case of implementing personalized education [10].

The current situation of a large number of students and few teachers and administrators increases Chinese universities' demands of big data to solve the dilemma of student management. The general situation of universities is that one manager needs to manage 150 to 200 students, and each teacher has 60 to 90 students in each course, even 120 in some cases. The big data could help teachers and administrators in different aspects, such as a list of students who need to focus by early warning system [11]. On the other hand, with low teacher-student ratio in China, big data analysis is undoubtedly a very effective way to improve personalized education and teaching.

3.2 Different Education Systems, Different Applications of Big Data in Education Management

In terms of management systems, Chinese universities adopt a system-managed student affairs management model for students, while American universities use a service-oriented management model featuring autonomy and democracy [12]. The different models have caused differences in the demand for big data in student management affairs. Chinese universities achieve strong control of students in accordance with the student management system, while American universities pay more attention to providing students with learning and living services. The application of big data in education management will reduce or optimize the teaching and management work in China, but provide students with various types of learning help in US.

The University of Kentucky in US introduced SAP's big data products in 2012. This platform provides all kinds of real-time information required by managers to help them make fast and scientific decisions. According to an IDC study, this big data product reduced the University of Kentucky's infrastructure costs by $201,000 and labor costs by $628,900 [13]. Public schools in Chicago have established an "Impact Management and Student Communication System" (IMPACT), which covers student information management, curriculum and teaching management, student service management, student performance statistics, home-school cooperation and other information [14]. The big data also supports schools in providing personalized services. In Beaverton School District, Oregon, school designs personalized behavior training programs for students' school life based on big data such as demographic data [15].

The application of management in Chinese colleges and universities is more flexible and diverse. For example, a university in Beijing applies big data to the management of college funding, which enables college funding management departments to analyze and screen students' big data information resources, which is more true and comprehensive. This enables Chinese colleges and universities to understand the funding targets, identify students in need of financial aid, and actively assist students in their lives [16]. The dining preferences data (like popular dishes and windows) provide a more scientific and reasonable suggestion for the improvement of related canteens [11]. In addition, some universities analyze data for early warning of abnormal situations like students failing to return to school at night. There are also universities that use network monitoring data to find out that those students who may be addicted to internet use provide early warning and implement timely intervention through student counselors.

Based on the above-mentioned application practices, we find out that big data in education in US has played an active role in regional and school education management. However, application hotspots in China are more focused on the monitoring and management of students. Many scholars have carried out related research or discussion on big data platforms at the school or regional level, but there are currently few systems that have actually entered the application stage.

3.3 Different Data Foundations Highlight Differences in Data Collection

US has a relatively complete system for the collection of big data in education. In terms of policy, the government has promoted a relevant legal system to guarantee such collection. In technology, the government cooperates with large companies in the computer field to provide technical support. The three-dimensional educational data network established covering the entire US, including national, state, school district, and school-level educational data systems at all levels. The school district or school needs to collect multiple types of data, determine the scope of the collected data, and determine the frequency of data collection [17].

At present, China has not formed a standard process for the collection of big data in education. Different schools collect data according to their own conditions. The national level collects data mainly through data reporting. The collected data is mainly basic education data, such as the number of students enrolled and graduates, the gross enrollment rate, the rate of advancement and the student-teacher ratio [18]. The types and scope of data collection vary widely between schools, and there is no sharing mechanism and platform for inter-school and inter-regional data. Data collection at the school level has certain advantages and flexibility since school can collect all kinds of student data in a comprehensive manner, such as student learning, life, behavior and other data, and establish school-level education within the school.

In summary, compared to US, China's big data in education is still in its infancy in terms of data collection. The collection of data is still in the situation of each university's own affairs. There are no regional or national big data in education institutions and platforms. However, in terms of the types of data collected internally by universities, the types of data that Chinese universities can collect are more abundant.

3.4 Different Attitudes Towards the Results of Big Data Analysis

The US government values the role of data in educational decision-making. In 1968, the Federal Department of Education established the "National Center for Education Statistics" (NCES), and published materials such as the "Education Statistics Yearbook" became an important basis for education decisions at all levels of government in US. The Education Science Reform Act (ESRA) passed in 2002 proposed that all educational policies must be supported by empirical data, thereby giving legislative power to data in educational decision-making.

The US government places particular emphasis on academic assessments when formulating education policies, such as the International Student Academic Assessment

(PISA), the Trends in International Mathematics and Science Study (TIMSS), and the National Assessment of Educational Progress (NAEP). Domestic assessments like NAEP not only allows policy makers to understand the overall status and trends of American education, but also analyzes the relationship between family background, education programs, and school teaching and student academic performance. This in turn affects federal and state education resource allocation and the funding and implementation of projects. In November 2015, the US Congress passed the "Every Student Succeeds Act" (ESSA), which adheres to the policy orientation of performance evaluation as an important basis for educational decision-making [19].

Chinese colleges and universities do not pay attention to the value of big data in education and believe that the development of big data in education costs money, time and effort [20]. Even a few universities have built big data platforms, they are not used for education decision-making or policy-making [21].

4   The Ethical Challenge of Big Data in Education

Big data technology, which is regarded as "changing science" [22], has gradually changed the education mode and promoted the sustainable and personalized development of teaching. However, it also produced a series of ethical issues.

4.1   Privacy Leak

In the process of analyzing massive learning data, big data in education technology has the potential to invade the privacy of students. The school or teachers did not obtain the consent of the students or their guardians when collecting, storing and using student data, or did not take measures such as obfuscation and anonymization to protect students' sensitive information: all of these hidden privacy violations. Due to the core demands of multiple use and cross-reuse of big data to maximize value, data miners often integrate and reorganize different types of student data. In this way, cross-checks of multiple data may be disclosed, the privacy of students will disappear unknowingly, and there will even be superimposed harm. For example, Bloom established a cooperative relationship with 9 states in US, and it can extract student data from different grades and attendance databases, with more than 400 data categories, including student name, address, assessment and attendance, disposition, and sensitive classification of family economic status, physical disability and mental illness. Despite the fundamental goal of the data collection is to promote personalized learning, the company finally has to close down [23, 24].

In China, the school can widely collect personal data of students by campus card, campus network and monitoring, and the data could be campus consumption, location information and web browsing records. Students have lost the right to know what kind of data is collected, and assure the privacy of their information [25]. In addition, students often exchange privacy information for convenience. For example, in order to obtain certain network services, they are forced to download some Internet plug-ins or network registration. In order to facilitate campus card recharging, students will associate campus cards with Alipay and bank cards. Unconsciously, students take the initiative to expose their privacy to operators and schools [26].

All kinds of data can be verified and explained to each other, and finally reproduce the individual's learning life and panorama, which is no different than "data surveillance" [27] that makes personal privacy impossible. Once these recorded data are leaked, it will be a great deal of personal privacy infringement, while people will inevitably suffer from the risk of privacy disclosure.

4.2 Data Dominance Imprisons Freedom

Data oriented decision-making will gradually wipe out students' creative thinking, resulting in the imprisonment of individual free development. The comprehensive education data will be used to predict students' future academic performance, and personalized education can be applied to improve students' learning. This is the reason why big data can promote revolutionary progress in the field of education [28].

In China, teachers can evaluate keywords based on dynamic data, and make accurate prediction and judgment on the development trend of students' public opinion and ideological behavior [29]. Teachers can also use the Internet and monitoring technology to capture and record the websites that students browse, the hot topic exchanges they participate in, and the micro blog logs they publish, so as to infer the development trend of individual behaviors. Based on the results of concept prediction, teachers can even carry out education intervention activities in advance, so as to reduce students' immoral behavior [30]. It is undeniable that this kind of accurate prediction does enhance the foresight and initiative of education, but its danger cannot be ignored, that is, it deprives students of their active choice and imprisons their free will.

In US, in the practice of "E-advisors" [31] and "Degree Compass" [9] that some schools are carrying out at present, the artificial judgment has been removed from the decision-making process to a large extent and replaced by the operation based on machine algorithm. People are programmed and will follow the principle of maximizing their benefits and minimizing their losses [32]. The system would make decision on changing majors for students when it recognized that students have low probability of achieving qualified results in a subject field, and students would have a difficult time to get rid of the predefined learning routes, and finally be the victims of probability prediction. In this sense, it causes the unfairness in education.

4.3 Historical Data Challenges Equity

The digital record based on big data is different from the memory of the human brain, there is no forgetting and interference, so what people see, hear, learn and experience will be completely preserved. At the same time, the permanent storage of massive learning behavior data will also mark the students with a fixed label, which makes them suffer from discriminatory treatment and challenges the fairness and justice of education. In the era of big data, data collection, storage and usage is more convenient and fast. Data may be extracted, analyzed or compared at any time, so it could be used as the basis of evaluation when entering or applying for a job, and put some implied "Electronic Labels" on the parties.

Many schools have set up electronic file bags [33] for students' moral development at different ages, which not only records the students' moral development and excellent moral behaviors, but also includes some moral irregularities such as cheating in examinations, bullying students and violating order. The bad digital record is like a shadow, which makes students sink into the mire of permanent memory. In a big data application, it is necessary to make a comprehensive record of the inappropriate behaviors made by students when their psychology is not mature, and take them as the main evaluation basis in the future decision-making.

5 Comparison of Privacy Protection of Big Data in Education Between China and US

5.1 Legal and Regulatory

The U.S. government has been working to strike a balance between the use of big data and the protection of privacy. As the White Paper states, "big data is changing the world. But it is not changing Americans' belief in the value of protecting personal privacy, of ensuring fairness, or of preventing discrimination [34]." Through various laws and regulations, US has basically established privacy protection legal system for a big data environment in education. At the federal government level, the Fourth Amendment to the US Constitution laid the legal cornerstone of privacy protection in US. In terms of protecting the privacy of students in the education field, US has successively introduced the "Children's Online Privacy Protection Rule (COPPA)", "Student Digital Privacy and Parental Rights Act (SDP-PRA)", and "Protection of Pupil Rights Amendment (PPRA)", "Children's Internet Protection Act (CIPA)" and other laws and regulations, as well as continuous amendments to the laws and regulations, in order to strengthen the legal protection of student privacy [23, 35]. At the state government level, data privacy protection has also received great attention recently. The data privacy protection legislation and related policies of each state are mainly reflected in the definition of the scope of protection of student data and specific measures to protect the privacy rights of students and parents. California alone has more than 25 privacy and data security laws. For example, the Colorado State Act 1294 (Colorado HB 1294) clearly defines the scope of permitted use of educational data and requires providers of educational data to protect student privacy during the use of the data [36].

In terms of legislation in China, there is currently no specific legislation on personal data protection. The protection of personal data is mainly reflected in decentralized legal regulations. In February 2013, the first personal information protection standard "Guidelines for the Protection of Personal Information of Information Security Technology, Public and Business Service Information Systems" was officially launched. The most significant feature of this standard is that before personal sensitive information is collected and used, it must be explicitly authorized [37]. The Network Security Law, which came into effect in 2017, is China's first legal regulation on personal information protection. It protects personal information as a special chapter and establishes a basic system for personal information protection. Although it has established a basic system for the protection of personal information, it is not a specific legislation for the protection of personal information. It is also different from the specially formulated personal information law. Secondly, the "Network Security Law" adopts the indirect protection principle for the protection of privacy rights. It protects the privacy rights by strengthening the protection of personal information, without directly mentioning the protection of privacy or privacy rights [38].

To sum up, we can see that there is no comprehensive personal privacy protection law in China, but US has established a set of legal system. There are big differences between China and US in the number and details of laws and regulations as well as in the concept of legislation.

5.2 Industry Self-discipline

Due to the complexity and diversity of privacy infringements in the era of big data, it is unrealistic to rely on laws and regulations for adjustment and regulation, and industry self-discipline is particularly important. Taking advantage of the flexibility and initiative of self-discipline organizations in the Internet industry and the education industry is an important part of protecting student privacy in the era of big data. US is a leader in the implementation of industry self-discipline, advocating the minimum intervention principle of "less government intervention, industry self-discipline [39]". Give more data privacy protection to the industry. The main industry specifications issued in the field of education are listed in the Table 2. The norms and initiatives of these industries make the privacy protection of big data in education in US be effectively guaranteed at the industry level.

China has not yet established a self-regulatory mechanism for the Internet industry, but various industries have gradually begun to establish industry norms. For example, the "Procedures for the Administration of Computer Information Network International Internet Security Protection", "Postal Law", "Banking Law" and other industry laws and regulations have formulated relevant measures for the protection of personal communications and mail data, industry-related information and data.

5.3 Protection Consciousness of Personal Privacy

National legislation and industry self-discipline are norms that rely on external forces. It is also of great significance for users to improve their awareness of rights protection and self-protection, and to actively take measures to avoid the leakage of personal privacy. In the sense of personal privacy protection, China has always lagged behind western countries. For example, there are almost no successful cases of infringement of personal information by internet enterprises in China. The reason is not only the lack of legislation and regulation, but also the lack of awareness of rights and self-protection of personal information. The popular WeChat social media in China exposes students' portraits, activities, addresses and other information to the network environment, which reflects that Chinese parents are in lack of understanding of students' privacy rights and awareness of privacy protection.

US regards privacy as a formal legal right and has a long history. Users, especially student parents, have a high degree of attention to privacy data. Not only do various laws and regulations provide students with special privacy protection, but also a special service department (Family Policy Compliance Office) is responsible for providing parents,

Table 2. Main industry specifications issued in the field of education

Issuer	Prescribed name	Main content
The software & information industry association (SIIA)	Student privacy pledge	"Not collect, maintain, use or share student personal information beyond that needed for authorized educational/school purposes" "Not sell student personal information" (https://studentprivacypledge.org/)
Future of privacy forum (FPF)	Policymaker's guide to student data privacy	Clarifies to parents the legal provisions related to the protection of students' data privacy, which institutions can use students' data under what circumstances, parents' rights in the protection of data privacy, and the corresponding legal appeal methods [40]
The software & information industry association (SIIA)	Best practices for the safeguarding of student in-formation privacy and security for providers of school services	Explains the purpose, transparency, school authorization, data security, data disclosure and other matters of education for service providers [41]

students and schools provide legal guidance on privacy protection, and accept complaints from parents and students, so that parents and students fully realize the importance of privacy and understand how to protect their privacy security (https://www.ed.gov/category/keyword/family-policy-compliance-office-fpco).

6 Analysis of the Reasons for the Differences of Big Data in Education Between China and US

Through the analysis of the above aspects, we can see that there are large differences in the application, ethics and privacy protection of big data in education between China and the US. The reasons could be differences in education systems, cultural concepts and technological developments between China and the US.

1. In terms of the education system, the relative lack of education resources in China makes the education and teaching activities focus on teachers and emphasize the centralized management mode. The application of educational big data is mainly used to solve the management difficulties caused by the large number of students and student affairs management needs under the centralized management mode. The

highly centralized student management mode provides the school more authority and autonomy in the data collection process, but the lack of regional or national data collection standards makes the data collection completely depend on the technical level of each school and the degree of emphasis on data. On the other hand, the US is rich in educational resources, which emphasizes student-centered education and adopts service-oriented management mode. Educational big data is mainly used in the process of education and teaching to provide students with diversified learning assistance. At the same time, the educational field has formed a relatively complete data collection standard from the national/regional school, and the data collection is more standardized.

2. The differences in historical development between China and the US have resulted in different or even opposite cultural concepts and values. The value of American culture is individualism, while that of China is collectivism [42]. This difference is also reflected in the differences in big data in education. The US has a strong understanding of individualism, which makes individuals pay more attention to the protection of their own data assets, and makes society pay more attention to the protection of individual data privacy. It also promotes the introduction of many laws on data privacy protection. Data privacy protection in the field of education has always been a hot topic of social concern. China's collectivist values make individuals pay less attention to individuality, have few sense of ownership of personal data assets. The whole society has a weak sense of privacy protection.

3. In terms of technology development, China's big data field is in its infancy. The nation and industry have begun to realize the importance of big data, but have not yet established data standards, forming national or regional data sharing norms and platforms. For example, some schools have begun to establish their own big data platforms, and some big data demonstration applications have emerged, although most of them are ephemeral. Big data in education in the US has entered a steady development stage. The perfect norms and the simultaneous development of the industry and legal protection system ensure the healthy development of the big data in education in the US. At the same time, the continuous application of big data by schools also promotes the development of big data. The training of big data talents is also subject to the overall technological development of big data. China lacks big data professionals, especially in the field of education, which is also an important factor in the failure of many big data applications and platforms. The US cultivates big data talents from universities, vigorously absorbs domestic and foreign big data talents in the field of scientific research, and cooperates with enterprises and scientific research institutions to cultivate comprehensive big data talents [43].

7 Conclusion

Through the analysis of this paper, we can see that both China and US have realized that the application of big data is an obvious advantage in promoting the development of education and an inevitable trend in the future. China and US have carried out relevant research and practical application. For China's big data in education, the overall development level lags behind that of US. There are many experience that can be used for reference in the development of big data in education, as follows:

1. At the national level, we should formulate data opening strategies and governance principles, build national big data platform, improve national and local education data governance institutions, and train professionals in big data field.
2. From the social level, we should promote data culture, vigorously promote big data governance, and strive to form a cultural atmosphere and era characteristics of "speaking with data, managing with data, making decisions with data, and innovating with data" in the whole society.
3. At all levels of educational institutions, we should build an application platform for big data in education, give full play to the advantages of big data mining and analysis technology, and constantly improve education and teaching, so as to promote the development of education.

In terms of big data privacy protection, US emphasizes industry self-discipline, weakens government intervention, and provides a widely accepted and constructive guidance paradigm for network privacy protection. Although a large number of national and local laws have been established, there is no comprehensive personal privacy protection law. At the same time, with the rapid development of big data, the revision and establishment of laws are facing the challenge of speed. China has a long way to go in big data privacy protection, including:

1. At the national government level, legislation is adopted to protect the right of personal network and data privacy.
2. Establish industry self-discipline mechanisms, and carry out special legislative protection for the financial, communication, logistics, education and other industries where privacy information overflows. Enterprises can collect and process data within the basic principles and framework, and provide targeted personalized services while protecting users' privacy information.
3. Enhance the individual's awareness of self-protection and rights protection, while respecting the network and data privacy of others.

In terms of the challenges faced by big data in education, China and US need to face the challenges of technology and ethics. In order to protect the rights and interests of data subjects, governments and multinational organizations including China and US have been actively seeking countermeasures. In recent years, great progress has been made in formulating relevant laws and regulations, establishing relevant ethical values or standards, and establishing relevant ethics committees.

The differences in big data in education between China and the US are fundamentally caused by the different educational systems, cultural concepts and technological development levels of the two countries. When we see the differences, we should also see that there are many similar steps in the development of big data between the two countries. For example, in the application direction of big data in education, although China and the US have different focuses, they are mainly applied in the four directions described in the paper. These similarities also determine the process of developing big data. We would recommend that both countries should learn from each other. Learning from the successful experience and failure lessons of other countries is an important measure to avoid detours. This is also the original intention of this research. In the future, we will continue to analyze and compare the big data in education of more countries, and provide more references for the development of big data. In the development and construction of big data in education, no matter what education system and basic conditions, we suggest to pay attention to the following points:

1. Attach importance to personnel training. In the field of education, especially in colleges and universities, there are unique talent conditions. In the process of developing big data, it will become an important factor for the success of education big data to cultivate big data talents of composite specialty in the field and improve students' data literacy.
2. Attach importance to data security. In the field of education, data mostly involves the privacy of minors, so data security is very important. Without strong data security, big data in education will not be able to move forward.
3. Attach importance to data openness. On the basis of protecting personal data, we should open more group data, make full use of scientific research and academic advantages in the field of education, encourage more educators and students to participate in the construction of big data in education.

References

1. UN Global Pulse: Big data for development: Challenges & opportunities. Naciones Unidas, Nueva York, mayo (2012)
2. Through Educational Data Mining: Enhancing teaching and learning through educational data mining and learning analytics: an issue brief. In: Proceedings of Conference on Advanced Technology (2012)
3. 国务院: 国务院关于印发促进大数据发展行动纲要的通知 (2015)
4. Mervis, J.: NSF director unveils big ideas. Science **352**, 755–756 (2016)
5. Villars, R.L., Olofson, C.W.: White Paper. Big Data: What It Is and Why You Should Care. Information Everywhere, But Where's The Knowledge (2014)
6. 唐斯斯,李冀红,杨现民: 发展教育大数据: 内涵,价值和挑战.现代远程教育研究 (2016)
7. 万圆: 试答钱学森之问: 加强高校师生互动—基于控制生师比和班级规模的探讨. 教育与考试 (2011)
8. 迈尔, 肯尼思, 库克耶维克托: 与大数据同行: 学习和教育的未来. 考试 (2015)
9. Denley, T.: Austin peay state university: degree compass. EDUCAUSE Review Online (2012). http://www.Educause.Edu/ero/article/austin-Peay-State-University-Degree-Compass
10. Munoz, C., Smith, M., Patil, D.J.: Big data: A report on algorithmic systems, opportunity, and Civil Rights. Executive Office of the President, May 2016
11. 曾浩, 李有增: 基于学生行为分析模型的高校智慧校园教育大数据应用研究. 中国电化教育 (2018)
12. 王蕾: 中美两国高校学生事务管理比较—以美国德克萨斯农工大学(TAMU) 与复旦大学为例. 山东英才学院学报 (2014)
13. University of Kentucky Leveraging SAP HANA to Lead the Way in Use of Analytics in Higher Education. https://www.techrepublic.com/resource-library/whitepapers/university-of-kentucky-leveraging-sap-hana-to-lead-the-way-in-use-of-analytics-in-higher-education/. Accessed 9 Jan 2020
14. Davis, C.S., John, E.S., Koch, D., Meadows, G.: Making academic progress: The University of Michigan STEM academy. Women in Engineering (2010)

15. West, D.M.: Big data for education: Data mining, data analytics, and web dashboards. Governance studies at Brookings (2012)
16. 刘畅: 大数据在高校精准资助管理工作中的应用探讨. 中国集体经济 (2018)
17. 柳海民, 郑燕林: 大数据在美国教育评价中的应用路径分析. 中国电化教育 (2015)
18. 年教育统计数据- 中华人民共和国教育部政府门户网站. http://www.moe.gov.cn/s78/A03/moe_560/jytjsj_2017/. Accessed 9 Jan 2020
19. 朱晓玲, 滕珺: 大数据在美国基础教育中的运用. 人民教育 (2014)
20. 毕瑞祥: 财政大数据建设策略研究. 中国管理信息化 (2019)
21. 杨铄: 论大数据与云计算对高校信息化的发展. 网络安全技术与应用 (2018)
22. Anderson, C.: The end of theory: the data deluge makes the scientific method obsolete. Wired Magazine (2008)
23. Regan, P.M., Jesse, J., Khwaja, E.T.: Big data in education: developing policy for ethical implementation in the US and Canada. In: presentation at the American Society for Public Administration Annual Conference, Seattle, WA. equalityproject.ca (2016)
24. Britz, J., Zimmer, M., Capurro, R.: The digital future of education. Int. Rev. Inf. Ethics (2014)
25. 王国琼: 大数据可视化对某高校学生行为分析的呈现 (2016)
26. 高峰: "大数据" 时代下的公民隐私权保护. 信息化建设 (2014)
27. 涂子沛: 数据之巅: 大数据革命, 历史, 现实与未来 (2014)
28. 薛孚, 陈红兵: 大数据隐私伦理问题探究. 自然辩证法研究 31, 44–48 (2015)
29. 郑琰: 大数据时代的高校德育: 从单一走向多元. 湖南师范大学教育科学学报 64–68 (2015)
30. 于颖: 大数据时代的学校德育: 机遇, 挑战及对策. 现代教育科学 98–100 (2015)
31. Luna, G., Medina, C.: Promising practices and challenges: e-advising special education rural graduate students. Rural Special Educ. Q. 26, 21–26 (2007)
32. Pitt, J.C.: Doing Philosophy of Technology: Essays in a Pragmatist Spirit. Springer, Dordrecht (2011). https://doi.org/10.1007/978-94-007-0820-4
33. 潘城: 基于网络的区域性学生电子档案袋评价的实践探索. 教育信息技术 38–40 (2013)
34. Executive Office of the President: Big Data: Seizing Opportunities, Preserving Values. Createspace Independent Pub (2014)
35. Weber, A.S.: The big student big data grab. Int. J. Inf. Educ. Technol. 6, 65 (2016)
36. Molnar, A., Boninger, F.: On the Block: Student Data and Privacy in the Digital Age–The Seventeenth Annual Report on Schoolhouse Commercializing Trends, 2013–2014. National Education Policy Center (2015)
37. 谢卫红, 樊炳东, 董策: 国内外大数据产业发展比较分析. 现代情报 20 (2018)
38. 张姗姗, 曾超: 中美教育大数据的对比研究. 世界教育信息 5 (2018)
39. Wikipedia contributors: Industry self-regulation. https://en.wikipedia.org/w/index.php?title=Industry_self-regulation&oldid=921538999. Accessed 9 Jan 2020
40. FPF Staff: Future of Privacy Forum Releases Policymaker's Guide to Student Data Privacy. https://fpf.org/2019/04/05/future-of-privacy-forum-releases-policymakers-guide-to-student-data-privacy/. Accessed 9 Jan 2020
41. Software & Information Industry Association: Best Practices for the Safeguarding of Student Information Privacy and Security for Providers of School Services, Software & Information Industry Association (2014). http://www.siia.net/Portals/0/pdf/siia_best_practices_for_student_info_privacy.pdf
42. 王俊霞: 美国的个人主义与中国的集体主义. 佳木斯大学社会科学学报 75–76 (2005)
43. 王晓明, 岳峰: 发达国家推行大数据战略的经验及启示. 产业经济评 15–21 (2014)

DLchain: Blockchain with Deep Learning as Proof-of-Useful-Work

Changhao Chenli, Boyang Li, and Taeho Jung[✉]

Department of Computer Science and Engineering, University of Notre Dame,
Notre Dame, IN 46556, USA
tjung@nd.edu

Abstract. Blockchains based on Proof-of-Work can maintain a distributed ledger with a high security guarantee but also lead to severe energy waste due to the useless hash calculation. Proof-of-Useful-Work (PoUW) mechanisms are alternatives, but finding hard puzzles with easy verification and useful results is challenging. Recent popular deep learning algorithms require large amount of computation resources due to the large-scale training datasets and the complexity of the models. The work of deep learning training is useful, and the model verification process is much shorter than its training process. Therefore, in this paper, we propose DLchain, a PoUW-based blockchain using deep learning training as the hard puzzle. Theoretical analysis shows that DLchain can achieve a security level comparable to existing PoW-based cryptocurrency when the miners' best interest is to maximize their revenue. Notably, this is achieved without relying on common assumptions made in existing PoUW-based blockchain such as globally synchronized timestamps. Simulated experiments also show that the extra network delay caused by data transfer and the full nodes' validation is acceptable.

1 Introduction

Blockchain is one of the distributed ledger technologies through which multiple users can reach a consensus without a trusted central authority. It also guarantees tamper-proofness for the stored records. Bitcoin [16] is the most successful application of blockchain and uses Proof-of-Work (PoW) as its consensus mechanism. Miners of Bitcoin need to perform many hash calculations as their proof and the system is secure unless the attacker has more than 50% hash power of the whole network. However, the energy consumption of Bitcoin mining has always been a concern of hash-calculation based blockchains. The estimated annual electricity consumption is above 70TWh, which is close to the annul electricity cost of Austria. Various consensus mechanisms have been proposed to mitigate the energy consumption in PoW, such as Proof-of-Stake (PoS) [12,17], Proof-of-Activity [4] and Proof-of-Authority [20]. While energy consumption is not an issue in these methods, their robustness is weaker than that of PoW [3,8,27]. Another approach is to replace the original hash puzzles in the PoW-based blockchains with useful computation tasks, which are known to be Proof-of-Useful-Work (PoUW) [32].

© Springer Nature Switzerland AG 2020
J. E. Ferreira et al. (Eds.): SERVICES 2020, LNCS 12411, pp. 43–60, 2020.
https://doi.org/10.1007/978-3-030-59595-1_4

In PoUW mechanisms, miners perform useful work for consensus, and the energy is not completely wasted since the performed work is useful.

In this paper, we propose DLchain, which uses the training process of deep learning (DL) as the hard puzzle to maintain a PoW-based blockchain. Two features make DL training suitable to be PoUW hard puzzle: (1) DL training needs a huge amount of calculation power and (2) the training process of DL (usually needs multiple rounds/epochs of feedforwarding) is much longer than its verification process (only one round/epoch). Such a PoUW mechanism may have good applications in real life. There are many open data platforms (e.g., open data platforms by governments and research institutions), and there are also platforms for online machine learning competitions (e.g., Kaggle). DLchain can be leveraged to allow miners to generate useful DL models out of such publicly available datasets and DL tasks.

There exist similar approaches [7,13], but both works rely on globally synchronized timestamps. This is a strong assumption in distributed systems because the time difference among miners can be large (e.g., up to 70 min in Bitcoin [14]). In DLchain, we remove such strong assumptions but still reach a security guarantee comparable to that of PoW-based blockchains. To do so, we introduce block-dependent randomness into the DL training as the seeds for pseudorandom functions used by the training algorithms. Doing so does not affect the training quality since we are modifying the seed of the functions instead of their output. In regular DL, when the model's accuracy reaches a certain level, further improving the accuracy becomes very hard. Currently, brute-force parameter tuning is used as a common method in reality [2,5], and it is also common that DL algorithms are trapped in some local minima or saddle points unless some random choices are made [15,25]. For example, stochastic jumping to other points in the parameter space is necessary to reach a better accuracy [21,33,34]. With more random jumps, one will have a better chance to further improve the model beyond such points. Therefore, improving models beyond the local minima or saddle points requires a large number of random trials [5,15,19]. Additionally, such trials are independent from each other and can be done in a distributed manner. From this observation, we can let miners perform random trials to keep finding DL models whose accuracy is higher than previous ones. Then, the trained DL model will serve as the proof of useful work.

This paper has the following contributions. First, we propose a new PoUW-based blockchain, DLchain, and the DL training process is different from existing PoUW blockchains using DL. Second, DLchain achieves enhanced security with weaker assumptions compared to existing approaches, which is comparable to that of PoW-based consensus. Namely, DLchain is secure if honest miners possess 67% of the computation power of the whole blockchain network. Finally, overhead of DLchain is acceptable even in the rare worst cases of the fork dilemma.

2   Related Works

Proof of Useful Work (PoUW): Recently, there has been attempts to replace the work in PoW with useful work, i.e., Proof-of-Useful-Work [32].

Primecoin [11] lets miners find prime chains for the proof. PoX [28] uses scientific calculations, e.g., matrix calculations, to replace the original hash calculation. Similarly, uPoW [1] also constructs their mechanism based on Orthogonal Vector problems, a problem that takes $n^{2-o(1)}$ time to be solved and approximately $O(n)$ time to be verified. However, the Cunningham chain found by miners in Primecoin are not known to have real applications; both PoX and uPoW assumes a central board to store the scientific/challenging problems, leading the system exposed to a potential risk of a single point of failure (SPoF). It is desired to a useful work who has real applications and is robust against collusion. Hybrid Mining [6] shares a similar idea with uPoW where miners solve NP-complete problems, aiming at a different problem compared to our system. Besides, since the problems in Hybrid Mining are submitted as special transactions, extra data transfer is reduced but the scalability of their problems is limited.

PoUW Combined with DL: There are two mechanisms that have been proposed to combine the DL field and blockchain. In Proof-of-Deep-Learning (PoDL) [7], each block's decision is divided into two phases. In Phase 1, a model publisher releases a desired model and a training dataset. Miners download the task and train the model. Before Phase 1 ends, miners calculate the hash values of their trained models and submit these as the commitments. At the beginning of Phase 2, the publisher release a test dataset and miners submit the block containing the models with the accuracy calculated from the test dataset. Submitted models' hash values must match the commitments in Phase 1. Full nodes select the block with the highest-accuracy model and append it to their blockchains. The data transmission in PoDL is too frequent, which impacts the throughput of the system. Besides, the released test datasets may be exploited by attackers in the future. More importantly, due to the settings of the two phases for each block interval, PoDL needs a synchronized timestamps, which hardly exist in PoW-based blockchains, and is therefore sensitive to the network delay. Li et al.'s work [13] addresses the data transmission issues and the released test datasets issues, however this is done by letting model publishers verify all submitted models. This is a bottleneck in terms of communication at the publisher's side, and this also results SPoF since the security relies on the publisher (Table 1).

Table 1. Comparison with Existing PoW/PoUW based systems

	PoW	PoX	Primecoin	uPoW	Hybrid Mining	PoDL	Li et al. [13]	Ours
Useful works?	✗	✓	○	✓	✓	✓	✓	✓
No SPoF?	✓	✗	✓	✗	✓	✗	✓	✓
No global clock?	✓	✓	✓	✓	✓	✗	✗	✓
Low network overhead?	✓	✗	✓	✓	✓	✗	✗	✗
No incentive to collude?	✓	✗	✓	✓	✓	✗	✗	✓
Efficient verification?	✓	✓	✓	✓	✓	✗	✗	✓

○: the usefulness of Cunningham chain is unknown.

3   System Model and Assumptions of DLchain

3.1   System Model of DLchain

There are three types of entities in DLchain.

Miners: Miners are the nodes in blockchains who participate in finding a new block. Instead of performing hash calculations for PoW, miners in DLchain perform DL training and submit trained models as the proof of useful work.

Full Nodes: Full nodes are the nodes who verify miners' blocks and maintain the blockchain. Accuracy verification of DL models is part of the block validation, and full nodes should be capable for this. Thus the minimum requirements for being full nodes in DLchain will be higher than those in PoW-based blockchains.

Task Publishers: Task publishers are the entities who are in charge of publishing DL training tasks to the system, which are similar to the open data platforms mentioned in Sect. 1. Different from previous works [7,13], there are multiple publishers publishing different tasks in DLchain, and the set of publishers will form a permissioned blockchain to store the order of these tasks. The consensus of this permissioned blockchain can be ensured by some CFT algorithms such as Raft [18], where a *leader* will be selected and other *followers* will follow the order decided by the leader. During each block interval, there will be only one task that both miners and full nodes focus on and they will move on to the next task when the current task is completed. Publishers can benefit from miners' trained models and they will need to store all the tasks (including other publishers' tasks) in case of a SPoF happens, e.g., a publisher may be overloaded when too many miners are downloading data from her/him. For each published task, its corresponding publisher will provide the model to be trained and a training dataset. Besides, the publisher will also specify a *Desired Accuracy*, so that the task can be terminated upon the trained model reaching such accuracy. Note that DLchain is a *hybrid − permission* blockchain, where the publishers set maintains a permissioned blockchain and other nodes (miners and full nodes) maintain a permissionless blockchain. The idea of combining different blockchain types comes naturally from the real-world scenario mentioned in Sect. 1.

3.2   Assumptions

Assumption 1: We assume improving the training accuracy (i.e., the accuracy measured from the training dataset) is meaningful work. Testing accuracy is a better metric for evaluating a model, but it is challenging to avoid attacks by greedy miners in the presence of test datasets unless secure globally synchronized timestamps exist [7,13]. Therefore, we focus on improving the training accuracy, and the test accuracy is not part of the DLchain design. Note that the models can still be useful. If the training dataset is very large and well-represents the real datasets, a model fitted to training dataset will have a good representation. Otherwise, the publishers can choose to measure the test accuracy of collected models on their own to find the best one for them.

Assumption 2: Usually, training accuracy growth is fast up to a certain threshold, after which it becomes stochastic. We will say there exists a threshold after which increasing the training accuracy becomes challenging and stochastic [5], and we call this threshold the *Difficulty Accuracy*. It is not easy to accurately infer the Difficulty Accuracy of a model, and we assume the publisher pre-trains the model the extent where s/he alone cannot further improve the training accuracy, and we treat the highest training accuracy achieved by the publisher as the Difficulty Accuracy. Then, we assume the training process after the Difficulty Accuracy involves stochastic/random search, without which significant improvement cannot be achieved [2,5]. Due to this, significantly improving the accuracy beyond *Difficulty Accuracy* has adequate hardness because it involves stochastic/random guesses over different hyper-parameters, but verifying whether a given model exceeds a certain level of accuracy is rather easy since one can perform a series of feed-forwarding without random guesses. With this assumption, the miners who can train more epochs have a better chance in finding a model with a higher training accuracy. Since s/he can perform more searching with more epochs. We can use the number of epochs trained per hour to characterize the training power of miners (denoted as *Epoch Rate*), and a miner with a higher Epoch Rate will be more likely to achieve better training accuracy.

Assumption 3: We assume the full nodes will have adequate computation power for verifying the accuracy of the submitted models by running feed-forwarding algorithms. This assumption is necessary in our system because of the different mechanisms we use to validate the miners' workload. This is a trade-off: we allow miners to perform DL training as the useful work in the PoUW, and the cost of this is that full nodes must be capable of calculating the accuracy of a model.

3.3   Attack Models

Denial-of-Service (DoS): Two potential types of DoS attacks will be considered: (1) malicious miners control multiple processes to download the published models from the miner, making the miner's server fail, and (3) malicious miners create multiple invalid blocks and fully occupy the full nodes to validate the fake blocks and eventually preventing the blockchain keep growing.

Model Stealing: In DLchain, as DL models are considered as the proof of useful work, malicious miners may try to reuse honest miners' models as their own proof when submitting new blocks.

Note that other common attacks in existing cryptocurrencies (e.g., double spending, fork generation) are prevented naturally with the safety and liveness properties described in Sect. 5.3. Besides, a potential selfish publisher attack will be discussed in Sect. 6.3.

4   Design of DLchain

4.1   Work Flow of DLchain (Fig. 1)

According to Fig. 1, the workflow of DLchain can be described as follows. In **step 1**, each publisher in the publisher set creates a task including a training dataset, a model pre-trained with the training dataset by her/himself, a *Desired Accuracy*, and a finite set of *Short-term Targets* which are accuracy thresholds. Publishers will broadcast their own tasks to other publishers and a list of tasks will be generated. All the publishers will maintain a permissioned blockchain where the order of the tasks to be published to the miners and full nodes will be stored. The consensus will be reached by leveraging Raft [18], where a publisher will be elected as the leader and all the other publishers will follow her/his decision of the order. (Note that any consensus mechanism can be used among the publishers. It is orthogonal to this paper which focuses on the PoUW-based consensus among full nodes and miners.) For each task, the *Short-term Targets* are introduced for the tasks whose completion (i.e., reaching the *Desired Accuracy*) will surely take longer time than the one block interval. These are chosen by the publisher such that reaching to the next *Short-term Target* from the previous one takes approximate the average time of block intervals. For instance, if the publisher provides a pre-trained model with an accuracy of 95% and the *Desired Accuracy* is 99%, s/he might set the *Short-term Targets* to be 97%, 98% and 98.5%. Similar to Bitcoin, block intervals with reasonable variance do not have security implications in DLchain. Tasks will be published by leveraging the idea of leader selection from Raft [18]. In **step 2**, miners and full nodes download the task. Note that miners can query arbitrary publishers and all the publishers can provide the access to downloading the task which was mentioned in Sect. 3.1. Miners will start DL training in **step 3**. Each miner either randomly chooses initial weights or copy the model in the previous block (pre-trained model in case the task just started). The miner then chooses any training algorithm on his/her own that requires *certain source of randomness* during the algorithm (e.g., SGD [24], Momentum [26], AdaGrad [9], Averaging [22] etc.,). Note that the DL training process in DLchain is different from normal training algorithms, which has been explained in Sect. 3.2. Usually, training algorithms involve some random choices during the training so that they can escape from the local minima or saddle points [2,5,29]. Towards this end, we abstract the training algorithm as $Train_x(M, D, S)$, where x determines the type of training algorithm, M is the model to be trained, D is the training dataset, and S is the seed for the randomness in the algorithm. After choosing the algorithm $Train_x$, the miner will perform the training using the model M, the training dataset D, and, most importantly, the root of the Merkle tree of all the transactions in the block plus the hash value of the previous block as the seed S for the random training algorithm $Train_x$. The need of this special seed will be explained further in Sect. 4.4. Once the model's training accuracy reaches the next Short-term Target, the miner stops the training. In **step 4**, a miner will first store the trained model at a publicly accessible place (e.g., cloud servers), generate a public link for downloading (similar to Li et al. [13]), and then include the link in the block header such that others can download the model. Other training-related information is also included in the link, including the specification of the training algorithm, initial weights, hyper-parameters, the length of training process, and any other information needed for reproducing the identical training process (denoted as *Training Parameters* hereafter). Anyone with the *Training Parameters* can reproduce the training results. Because the Merkle tree root is used as the seed S in $Train_x(M, D, S)$, once the same *Training Parameters* are used for the training, exactly identical training process can be reproduced from the training algorithm. We assume signature schemes are in place to guarantee the integrity of the block, but we omit the description of signatures for simplicity. Note that the block header does not contain a nonce, and the block header's hash does not need to be small. In **step 5**, full nodes will use the link in the header to download the model and compute the training accuracy after receiving a block. The decision of whether the block is valid will be made based on the block acceptance policy (to be described in Sect. 4.3) in **step 6**. Besides existing validation in Pow-based blockchains, full nodes validate whether the training accuracy of a block's model exceeds the lowest unreached *Short-term Target*. If not, the block is discarded. In other words, the *Short-term Targets* determine the difficulty of block mining. As is shown in **step 7 & 8**, both miners and full nodes continuously check whether any one of the *Termination Conditions* is met: a task is terminated when full nodes receive a model whose training accuracy exceeds the *Desired Accuracy*; or, a task is terminated when the *Deadline* has passed. The Deadline is the time defined by DLchain, which stops a task that is lengthy. If the conditions are not satisfied, the miners continue the same task. Otherwise, the task is terminated and the next task will be retrieved from the publishers.

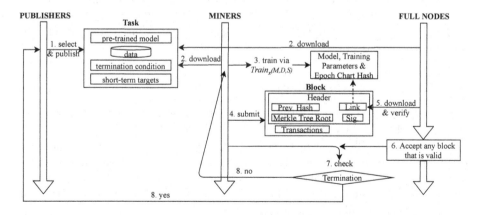

Fig. 1. Work flow of DLchain.

4.2   Mining via Training

After the publisher broadcasts a task to the network, both miners and full nodes download the contents of the task. Every miner then starts to train the model by using his/her own $Train_x(M, D, S)$ with independently chosen x, M, S, which is the mining process of DLchain. In other words, the miners choose the training algorithm x, initial weights and the hyper-parameters (e.g., batch size, learning rate decay function) that define the model M arbitrarily based on their needs, and start the training process with the training dataset and the seed S, which is the Merkle tree root of the transactions plus the hash value of the previous block. Note that there are random choices during the training (e.g., data loading in the mini-batch or adjustment of learning rate) and the randomness comes from pseudorandom functions with the seed S. The miners will submit their blocks when the training accuracy of their models reaches a lowest unreached Short-term Target. The purpose of fixing the seed during the training is to achieve exact reproducibility at the full nodes' side, which will be part of the validation in case forks occur. Fixing the seed in the training does not affect the quality of training as long as the pseudorandom functions are random enough. The seed used by the training algorithm is the Merkle tree root and the previous block's hash vlue, which are both the digest of a cryptographic hash that is usually 256 bits or more. Therefore, using the Merkle tree root as the seed does not decrease the degree of randomness required by existing training algorithms.

Miners also collect the accuracy values for every epoch during the training. We call a chart showing the value for each epoch *Epoch Chart*. They also calculate the several hash values based on the Epoch Chart of the sequence and the Merkle tree root of the transactions, and include these hash values, denoted as *Epoch Chart Hash* hereafter, into the downloadable link in the header to achieve security against attackers who attempt to steal the published models. To be specific, the number of hash values calculated based on the Epoch Chart is relevant to the number of epochs that the miner trains, e.g., miners should calculate a hash value every time they train 100 epochs. Relevant security analysis can be found in the next section.

4.3   Block Acceptance Policy

For each block (in the order of the arrival), full nodes download the model using the link and verify whether the training accuracy of the model exceeds any lowest unreached Short-term Target besides all other trivial block validation (e.g., validity of transactions and signatures). If all are verified correctly, full nodes accept the block; otherwise, they discard the block and validate the next one. If more than one block is valid, which means a fork has appeared, the full nodes will keep all valid blocks at the same block height.

Since the block contains the link to the model, attackers may try to steal others' models to generate a new block at the same height, hoping to create a fork and potentially gain the block reward. To thwart such attackers, if multiple blocks appear at the same height, the full nodes further reproduce the training process of each model in order to check whether the corresponding miner has conducted work correctly, for which we have defined and used the Epoch Chart Hash as aforementioned (Sect. 4.2). First, they retrieve the Training Parameters using the link in the corresponding block, and use the Merkle tree root and the previous hash in the block as the seed S to rerun $Train_x(M, D, S)$. After rerunning the same training process using the same Training Parameters, full nodes calculate the Epoch Chart Hash consecutively as described in Sect. 4.1 and make the comparison when each hash value is calculated. Note that the Epoch Chart Hash is deterministic and dependent only on the Training Parameters (which includes training lengths) and the seed used to draw the pseudorandomness in the training algorithm. Then, if the all the hash values of calculated Epoch Chart Hash, which can be considered as the *checkpoints* of the Epoch Chart, are identical to the ones in the block, the block is deemed valid. Otherwise, if any of the calculated Epoch Chart Hash is different, the block and the corresponding fork is discarded. Note that the setting of multiple hash values indicate the idea of *checkpoint* so as to eliminate the extra verification that full nodes have to perform. There is a trivial trade-off between the interval of two checkpoints and the granularity of the check. The interval setting of 100 epochs is just for explanation and such setting can be left to users in real-world application. If multiple blocks at the same height are all valid, they form valid forks, and consensus is derived with our novel *point system* in the next section.

4.4   Fork Resolution via Novel Point System

When several blocks arrive at the same height, a fork appears, and this is common in any blockchain. Whenever a fork appears and they are all valid, DLchain uses a *point system* to decide which fork is the main chain. Namely, DLchain gives each valid block one point, and the fork with the most points is accepted by the full nodes as the main chain. If there are multiple forks with the same points, the longest chain with the most blocks are accepted as the main chain. In case of a tie, the tie is broken by the miners, who are motivated to choose the fork that appeared earlier. This seems identical to the mechanism in PoW-based cryptocurrency that takes the longest chain as the main chain, however the following extra rules result in an important difference.

Rule 1: Every Short-term Target grants at most one point in DLchain, and a block earns one point only when its model exceeds multiple *Short-term Targets* at once. In other words, if a block contains a model whose accuracy is extremely high and exceeds several unreached *Short-term Targets* at the same time, the block earns only one point.

Rule 2: If multiple valid blocks are submitted to compete for the point of the same Short-term Target (e.g., multiple valid blocks are submitted for the same Short-term Target), the block containing the Training Parameters that indicate the longest training process (i.e., the most number of epochs) earns the point.

Rule 1 seems counterintuitive because it seems to penalize the miner who consumed an excessive amount of resources to achieve a much better model, but it is exactly the opposite. We show this using the following theorem.

Theorem 1: *The fork maintained by rational honest miners, whose motivation is to maximize the block rewards they receive, gains the most points in DLchain.*

Proof: The maximum points that any fork can get from this task is thus equal to the number of the *Short-term Targets* defined by the task. We will show that the fork maintained by rational honest miners will gain the maximum points from this task. Note that DLchain grants only one point even if a model exceeds multiple unreached *Short-term Targets* at once. Then, suppose the next unreached *Short-term Target* is 95% and an honest miner X finds his/her model's accuracy is 96.1%, which exceeds two unreached *Short-term Targets*, 95% and 96%. We claim that the best choice for her/him will be to keep training to see whether her/his model's accuracy could fall a little below 96% so that her/his block can gain the point for reaching 95%. The miner will not wait for the other miner's model reaching 95% because her/his model does not include that miner's block hash value as a part of the random seed. Also, the miner will not publish her/his model directly. As is mentioned in Rule 1, if a model exceeds more than one Short-term Target, its corresponding block can only get one point, Therefore, s/he needs to take the risk of losing the competition, because a new fork that contains two blocks for both 95% and 96% must gain an extra point when competing with the existing block. All rational miners will thus choose to wait for someone else's block if their models exceed two *Short-term Targets* at the same time. The same analysis holds for the models exceeding more than two *Short-term Targets*, and all rational miners will always ensure that the chain they work on will reach the *Short-term Targets* one by one without skipping any one. Therefore, the fork maintained by rational honest miners gain the most points in DLchain.

Thus, honest miners will always submit the block as soon as their training accuracy exceeds the lowest unreached Short-term Target.

Rule 2 is introduced to thwart the attackers who attempt to steal an honest miner's model (via the public link) and perform short-period training on it. If only short-period training is performed on the model, then no matter what seed is used, the accuracy is not likely to change significantly, and the full nodes are unable to tell with confidence whether the given model with an extremely short training period is derived from a stolen model or purely by coincidence. Therefore, we give the point only to the model whose training process has the most number of epochs among all the competing models, making it unlikely that the attackers can generate a valid block efficiently by stealing others' models.

Most importantly, this point system of DLchain allows full nodes to make decentralized decisions on submitted models without relying on globally coordinated timestamps, which is a significant improvement compared to similar works [7,13].

4.5   Termination Conditions of Tasks

The publisher sets a *Desired Accuracy* for the task when creating it, and the protocols of DLchain define a Deadline for all tasks. In case the publisher's *Desired Accuracy* or *Short-term Targets* are too high, miners may keep performing DL training by wasting energy. To avoid this, a task that does not reach *Desired Accuracy* before Deadline is terminated by full nodes (i.e., moving on to the next task). This deadline can be adjusted in a way similar to the way difficulty of hash calculation is adjusted in PoW-based blockchains. Namely, we can adjust the Deadline such that the average length of each task is a constant.

5   Mechanism Analysis

5.1   Natural Forks at the Top

When multiple blocks are submitted at the top height (e.g., several blocks submitted almost at the same time by coincidence), only the block with the most number of epochs will be kept, and the consensus can be derived. Rational honest miners will be motivated to discard the current work and continue from a newly discovered block since trying to replace the current block does not help them. At best they can steal the point from an existing block, but other miners who have already started working on the next block will find the next block faster, and the two forks now have the same points. When a tie happens, full nodes choose the longer fork, so the fork created by other miners will become the main chain and the rational honest miners who tried to replace the latest block gets nothing.

5.2   Double Spending via Normal Training and 67% Security

Double spending is an attack where the attacker tries to override existing blocks by creating a fork starting from a past block. To launch it in DLchain, an attacker needs to generate a fork starting from several blocks behind and try to get the same points as the main chain. One choice for the attacker is to normally train the models, improve the model's training accuracy, and generate the blocks by following the rules of DLchain. In this case, the attacker can successfully double spend when s/he catches up with the main chain in terms of the points (which is equal to the number of valid blocks if honest miners are rational).

To do so, for every block starting from where the fork starts, s/he will need to generate a model using his/her own seed (which affects the whole training process) such that (1) the model's accuracy exceeds the lowest unreached Short-term Target as of the corresponding block height and (2) the training process has more epochs than the other model in the main chain at the same height. The rationale for these are obvious: the attacker needs to gain points by winning over an already-accepted block (and thus the accepted blocks lose the points).

Note that the analysis of Bitcoin [16] shows that double spending attacks are thwarted if honest miners grow the main chain faster than the attackers do, because the attackers can never catch up with the main chain. Similarly, the following theorem explains the security guarantee of DLchain.

Theorem 2: *If the group of honest miners grows the main chain at least twice as fast as the attackers do, DLchain is robust against double spending attacks.*

Proof: Suppose the point of the honest miners' chain is P_h, the point of the attackers' chain is P_a and the difference of two chains is $d = P_h - P_a \geq 0$. If the attackers successfully create a valid block in the past, then P_a will be increased by one and P_h will be decreased by one. Such change is caused by the point system since at the same block height, full nodes will only give one point to one chain and no point to other chains (Sect. 4.4). At this time, the difference between two parties will become $(P_h - 1) - (P_a + 1) = d - 2$. However, as is supposed that the honest group's chain grows at a speed that is twice of the speed of the attackers' chain, the honest group must have appended at least two more blocks while the attackers create one valid block. Thus, P_h will be increased by two and the new difference between two parties will be $d' = ((P_h - 1) + 2) - (P_a + 1) = d$, which makes the difference keep the same. Since the main chain started with more points, the main chain will always have the maximum points in this case, and DLchain is robust against double spending attacks.

Therefore, we claim that if the group of honest miners possess at least 67% of the total calculation power (denote as Epoch Rate hereafter) of the entire network, DLchain can thwart double spending attacks with a high probability. Compared to Bitcoin's 51% security, we need honest parties to have more than 67% of the entire network's Epoch Rate. This means the assumption of our system is stronger, but this is a reasonable trade-off since the proof of DLchain is deep learning models, which is more useful than that the hash values.

Next, we estimate whether honest miners can grow the main chain at least twice as fast as the attackers in practice. Note that a rigorous analysis is challenging because (1) it is hard to compare the quality of different training algorithms, and (2) there is no real data showing the Epoch Rate of the hardware. We simplify the case to assume everyone uses the same training algorithm and rely on user-provided benchmark data of graphic cards to give a rough estimate. The purpose of this is to understand whether honest miners can realistically grow the main chain at least twice as fast as attackers rather than under what exact circumstances honest miners can do so. To do so, we consider a conservative setting where the attackers have the most powerful hardware and the honest users have modest hardware.

As of December 2019, the best GPU for DL is arguably the NVIDIA TITAN V. In contrary, NVIDIA GTX 970 can be considered as a modest GPU (released in the market 5 years ago). The user-provided benchmark data for these two NVIDIA video cards show that, the best performance that a TITAN V can achieve is 4 times of the GTX 970's worst performance [31], with which we make a rough conjecture that the Epoch Rate of TITAN V is 4 times of that of GTX 970 when the same training algorithm is used.

Even in such a conservative setting, one GPU card of attackers can be at most 4 times faster than one GPU card of the honest miners. In other words, for the attackers to be able to launch the double spending attack in this setting, the number of the GPU cards attackers need to have should be at least 1/8 of the GPU cards possessed by the honest group of miners. We conjecture that it is realistic to assume honest miners possess at least 8 times as many GPU cards as attackers do. Unfortunately, due to the lack of real data, we are unable to give a more rigorous analysis than this rough estimate.

5.3   Safety Properties and Liveness Properties

We use the *safety* and *liveness* [10,23] to describe the security of DLchain.

Safety property 1: *Publication Safety:* *If the publisher of the published task is failed, miners can still download and train the task, which the DDoS attack on publisher can be prevented.*
This property is ensured by the fact that all the publishers will form a permissioned blockchain and reach a consensus on the current published task. Each publisher will also store all other publishers' tasks and provide the access to downloading the task (Sect. 3.1).

Safety property 2: *Model Safety:* *Model stealing will not happen in DLchain.*
This property can be ensured by referring to the Sect. 4.3 since malicious miners cannot directly reuse other miners' models due to the check of Epoch Chart Hash.

Liveness property 1: *Task Termination:* *If a task is chosen to be published, then the task will be completed within a certain amount of time which was pre-defined by its termination conditions.*
This property can be ensured by combining the termination conditions set by the publisher and the deadline set by the system Sect. 4.5. Such property will help the system avoid trapping in a single task whose desired accuracy is too high to be reached.

Liveness property 2: *Consensus:* *Among all the publishers, if the honest publishers are more than $\frac{2}{3}$ and the honest miners posses more than $\frac{2}{3}$ of the total Epoch rate of the system, then there will be only one chain (that contains the most calculation power) in* DLchain.
The consensus can be ensured by combining the publisher selection (Sect. 3.1), block acceptance policy (Sect. 4.3) and the fork resolution via point system (Sect. 4.4). With these factors ensured, during the whole time of the system, each task can be selected and published, miners can download and train the task, model stealing can be prevented and fork can also be resolved. Such trails can therefore lead to a carefully designed PoUW blockchain and reach a consensus.

As for other two types of DDoS attacks, either on miner's submission or on full nodes' validation, the key point of these attacks are highly relevant to the size of the proof. In fact, Bitcoin system also faces similar situations such as malicious miners will randomly generate a lot of invalid blocks to let the full nodes verify them and such DDoS attack is hard to succeed in Bitcoin system since the verification speed on hash values is really fast. In DLchain, on the other hand, the size of the model will take a significant role when comes to such attacks. Namely, the smaller the size of the model, the closer security level in defending DDoS DLchain will have compared to that of Bitcoin. In addition, with the help of Epoch Chart Hash as the checkpoints when solving the fork dilemma, the computation burden on full nodes will be decreased.

6   Discussions

6.1   Block Size and Block Intervals

Because DLchain requires various entities to exchange datasets and models whose size is measured in gigabytes, the network delay when transferring the dataset among the system is non-negligible. Therefore, the block intervals in DLchain should also be extended so that the network delay caused by data transferring (e.g., task downloading and model submission) is negligible compared to the block intervals. We do not discuss an appropriate interval in this paper, as that is orthogonal to the design proposed in this paper. However, only extending the block interval without increasing the original block size will influence the throughput of our system. Thus, we stress that the block size should grow linearly *w.r.t.* the defined block intervals to not decrease the transaction throughput. We ran a sample DL training [30] on two Quadro RTX 6000 GPUs to demonstrate the relationship between the network delay caused by data transferring and the block intervals. The total time for downloading the project (including both the model and the dataset) is less than 5s. We perform 100 epochs on the left chart, 50 epochs on the right chart and each epoch takes about 30s to be finished. As is shown in left chart of Fig. 2, the training accuracy starts to increase slowly after 20 to 30 epochs. Each point on the red line denotes an acceptable model whose training accuracy exceeds the next Short-term Target and there are around 20 epochs between each two red points. Compared to the time for downloading (equals to the data transfer overhead), the training process (equals to the block interval) is much longer, which means the network delay caused by data transfer is negligible compared to the block intervals. Also, the time of accuracy validation needs one epoch, which is also much less than that of the training process. Similar conclusion can also be made when considering the right chart where the block intervals are reduced to around 10 epochs (approximately 5 min). Note that this sample training is just for demonstration and in the real-world scenario. We argue that the time for both network delay caused by the data transfer and the block interval mainly determined by the DL training will increase proportionally since the datasets can be larger and the models can be more complex. Besides, for those DL training whose training time is short, we can increase the difference between *Short-term Targets* so that the block intervals can still be much longer than the network delay.

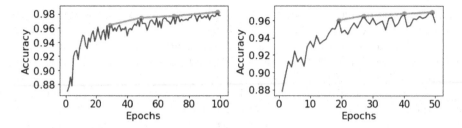

Fig. 2. Sample DL training examples.

6.2   Extra Overhead

Extra Overhead of the Publisher: The publisher needs to pre-train his/her model before creating a task, which is an acceptable computation overhead because, after then, s/he can leverage the distributed computation provided by the miners for further improvements.

Extra Overhead of Full Nodes: Compared to the full nodes in PoW-based blockchains, full nodes in DLchain need to additionally download the dataset and the model for block validation. This incurs a non-negligible network overhead, however the dataset downloading occurs once only for each task, and this can happen in advance before the task starts. Also, the model can be as large as several GBs, however the block intervals can be adjusted accordingly so that the model transfer via network is negligible. Full nodes in DLchain also have extra computation overhead, including (1) calculating the models' accuracy; (2) rerunning the training process when solving forks; (3) generating the Epoch Chart while training; (4) some extra hash calculations such as the Epoch Chart Hash. (1) is accepted as only one round of feedforwarding is involved. (2) does take some time, but the load can be eliminated by applying several checkpoints in the Epoch Chart Hash (more details in Sect. 4.2). (3) is merely the accuracy logging, and (4) is hash calculation, which are negligible compared to (1).

Extra Overhead of Miners: Miners experience extra network overhead compared to those in PoW-based blockchains, and it is almost identical to that of full nodes. Some extra computation needs to be done by miners in DLchain, which includes: (1) training the model; (2) generating the Epoch Chart while training; (3) calculating the Epoch Chart Hash; (4) generating signatures. We are using the DL training to replace the hash puzzles as the useful work in DLchain, therefore the training process itself is a necessary workload leading to meaningful applications rather than the extra overhead. Similar to the analysis for the full nodes, (2) and (3) are negligible compared to the training, and (4) is negligible as well.

6.3   Selfish Publisher Attack

A potential *selfish publisher attack* may happen where a malicious publisher will pre-train her/his task to reach one or more Short-term Targets and release the corresponding block(s) after her/his task is selected by the set of publishers, in which case the publisher can earn block rewards. Due to the nature of Internet, we cannot prevent a publisher from being a miner at the same time. The malicious publisher can launch such attack in two ways, either setting some Short-term Targets which can be reached easily or training for a long time to reach some high Short-tern Target(s). For the first way of attack, the publisher can generate *valid* blocks with appropriate models in a short time. When several continuous blocks are submitted in a short time, the blocks will be discarded. This is because too short intervals indicate the difficulty of the task in low, whereas DLchain considers a scenario where improving model accuracy is very hard after the Difficulty. On the other way, the malicious publisher can train the model on her/himself for a long time and generate the blocks. However, as we assumed in Sect. 3.2 that the accuracy improvement after the Difficulty Accuracy is *really* hard, the cost to launching such attack can be relative high in reality. Actually, in this case, the miner is trying to compete with the whole network's computation power. Therefore, even though we cannot prohibit this type of attack, the incentive for a malicious publisher to do so will be restricted by the trade-off between the resources consumption and the benefit earned from block rewards.

7 Conclusion

In this paper, we proposed DLchain, a PoUW-based blockchain that uses DL training as the hard problem. DLchain provides a new environment for leveraging the distributed computing resources of blockchain miners to improve better training accuracy of a model. Our extensive analysis shows that the consensus of DLchain is comparable to that of PoW-based consensus in terms of the robustness, and it has several significant improvements compared to similar work that attempts to build blockchain on top of DL. We also described the safety and liveness properties and sample experiment results also show that our system is practical. Some limitations related to selfish publisher attacks are identified, and practical analysis is also made.

References

1. Ball, M., Rosen, A., Sabin, M., Vasudevan, P.N.: Proofs of useful work. IACR Cryptology ePrint Archive, 2017:203 (2017)
2. Bardenet, R., Brendel, M., Kégl, B., Sebag, M.: Collaborative hyperparameter tuning. In: ICML 2013, pp. 199–207 (2013)
3. Barinov, I.: Proof of Stake Decentralized Autonomous Organization
4. Bentov, I., Lee, C., Mizrahi, A., Rosenfeld, M.: Proof of activity: extending bitcoin's proof of work via proof of stake. IACR Cryptology ePrint Archive 2014:452 (2014)
5. Bergstra, J., Bengio, Y.: Random search for hyper-parameter optimization. J. Mach. Learn. Res. 13(Feb), 281–305 (2012)

6. Chatterjee, K., Goharshady, A.K., Pourdamghani, A.: Hybrid mining: exploiting blockchain's computational power for distributed problem solving. In: SAC 2019, pp. 374–381. ACM (2019)
7. Chenli, C., Li, B., Shi, Y., Jung, T.: Energy-recycling blockchain with proof-of-deep-learning. arXiv preprint arXiv:1902.03912 (2019)
8. "Fake Stake" Kernel Description, February 2019. https://bit.ly/2Txk146
9. Duchi, J., Hazan, E., Singer, Y.: Adaptive subgradient methods for online learning and stochastic optimization. J. Mach. Learn. Res. **12**(Jul), 2121–2159 (2011)
10. Dziembowski, S., Eckey, L., Faust, S.: Fairswap: how to fairly exchange digital goods. In: ACM SIGSAC, pp. 967–984 (2018)
11. King, S.: Primecoin: Cryptocurrency with Prime Number Proof-of-work, vol. 1, p. 6, 7 July 2013
12. King, S., Nadal, S.: PPCoin: Peer-to-Peer Crypto-currency With Proof-of-Stake. Self-published paper, 19 August 2012
13. Li, B., Chenli, C., Xu, X., Jung, T., Shi, Y.: Exploiting computation power of blockchain for biomedical image segmentation. In: CVPR 2019 Workshops (2019)
14. Lopp, J.: Bitcoin timestamp security, July 2019. https://bit.ly/332n877
15. Loshchilov, I., Hutter, F.: SGDR: Stochastic gradient descent with warm restarts. arXiv preprint arXiv:1608.03983 (2016)
16. Nakamoto, S., et al.: Bitcoin: A Peer-to-Peer Electronic Cash System (2008)
17. Nxt whitepaper. https://nxtwiki.org/wiki/Whitepaper:Nxt, journal=Nxt
18. Ongaro, D., Ousterhout, J.: In search of an understandable consensus algorithm. In:U SENIX ATC, vol. 14, pp. 305–319 (2014)
19. O'donoghue, B., Candes, E.: Adaptive restart for accelerated gradient schemes. Found. Comput. Math. **15**(3), 715–732 (2015)
20. Paritytech.   paritytech/parity-ethereum,   July   2019.   https://github.com/paritytech/parity/wiki/Proof-of-Authority-Chains
21. Perkins, T.J.: Reinforcement learning for pomdps based on action values and stochastic optimization. In: AAAI/IAAI, pp. 199–204 (2002)
22. Polyak, B.T., Juditsky, A.B.: Acceleration of stochastic approximation by averaging. SIAM J. Control Optim. **30**(4), 838–855 (1992)
23. Ramachandran, G.S., et al.: Trinity: a byzantine fault-tolerant distributed publish-subscribe system with immutable blockchain-based persistence. In: ICBC, pp. 227–235. IEEE (2019)
24. Robbins, H., Monro, S.: A stochastic approximation method. Ann. Math. Stat. **22**, 400–407 (1951)
25. Ruder, S.: An overview of gradient descent optimization algorithms. arXiv preprint arXiv:1609.04747 (2016)
26. Rumelhart, D.E., Hinton, G.E., Williams, R.J., et al.: Learning representations by back-propagating errors. Cogn. Model. **5**(3), 1 (1988)
27. Saleh, F.: Blockchain Without Waste: Proof-of-Stake. Available at SSRN 3183935 (2019)
28. Shoker, A.: Sustainable blockchain through proof of exercise. In: NCA, pp. 1–9. IEEE (2017)
29. Snoek, J., Larochelle, H., Adams, R.P.: Practical Bayesian optimization of machine learning algorithms. In: NIPS, pp. 2951–2959 (2012)
30. Tencent. Tencent/neuralnlp-neuralclassifier, April 2020
31. Nvidia gtx 970 vs titan v. https://bit.ly/3aFwVCQ
32. Wang, W., et al.: A survey on consensus mechanisms and mining strategy management in blockchain networks. IEEE Access **7**, 22328–22370 (2019)

33. Williams, R.J.: Simple statistical gradient-following algorithms for connectionist reinforcement learning. Mach. Learn. **8**(3–4), 229–256 (1992)
34. Young, S.R., Rose, D.C., Karnowski, T.P. Lim, S.-H., Patton, R.M.: Optimizing deep learning hyper-parameters through an evolutionary algorithm. In: MLHPC 2015, p. 4. ACM (2015)

Blockchain Federation Enabled Trustable Internet of Things

Zhitao Wan[1], Minqiang Cai[2(✉)], Xiuping Hua[1,3(✉)], Jinqing Yang[2], and Xianghua Lin[2]

[1] University of Nottingham Ningbo China and Ningbo Free Trade Zone Blockchain Laboratory, Ningbo, China
xiuping.hua@nottingchain.com
[2] Institute of Advanced Technology Research, Ge Lian Corporation, Hangzhou, China
cai@ge-lian.com
[3] Nottingham University Business School China, University of Nottingham Ningbo China, Ningbo, China
xiuping.hua@nottingham.edu.cn

Abstract. The Internet of Things (IoT) provides an infrastructure enabling advanced functions based on interoperable information and communication technologies by interconnecting physical and virtual things. IoT has gained more and more attention from both academy and industry. However, the design, maintenance, and governance of IoT are facing challenges because of an enormous amount of heterogeneous devices involved. IoT requires strengthening its trustable features. The blockchains are immutable distributed ledger systems supporting trustable features including security, scalability, privacy, safety, and connectivity usually without a central authority. Due to the complexity of IoT system any current blockchain cannot satisfy all demands of heterogeneous devices, networks, and higher level functionalities. This paper proposes a novel reference architecture combines Blockchain Federation with IoT to make IoT capable of being trusted. The architecture enables trustable features by integrating blockchains with different IoT tiers and layers. Proof of concept system is implemented to demonstrate the correctness and feasibility of the architecture. Furthermore, the future directions of Blockchain Federation and IoT evolution are discussed.

Keywords: Blockchain Federation · Internet of Things (IoT) · Trustable

1 Introduction

The IoT is expanding in a fast track and reports predict that the number of IoT devices will skyrocket in the range of around several billion to more than fifty billion by 2020 and is far more than the laptops, desktops, tablets and smartphones. IoT is applied to a broad spectrum of scenarios like personal accessories, house appliances, healthcare, smart homes, smart cities, supply chain management, manufacturing, identity management and access control, electricity market systems, insurance systems, and etc. [1]. IoT

© Springer Nature Switzerland AG 2020
J. E. Ferreira et al. (Eds.): SERVICES 2020, LNCS 12411, pp. 61–76, 2020.
https://doi.org/10.1007/978-3-030-59595-1_5

benefits organizations including operational efficiency, better customer experiences and enhanced business models.

With the increased adoption of IoT, the devices give new opportunities for hackers to launch attacks of unprecedented scale and impact. There are so many devices in IoT and owners may not even be aware that they have them. These attacks can be designed to install ransomware, invade privacy or even take control of the device to launch secondary attacks on organizations through distributed denial-of-services (DDoS) attacks.

Many challenges prevent the securing of IoT devices and ensuring security in an IoT environment. Because the emerging IoT devices are relatively new, security has not always been considered top priority during a product's design phase. Additionally, because IoT is a nascent and vibrant market, many product designers are function driven and manufacturers are more interested in getting their products to market quickly, rather than taking the necessary steps to build security in from the start. Moreover, most of the IoT devices are low power consuming embedded devices with limited memory, flash size, computing capacity and internetworking bandwidth. These also restrict the integration of security related function. IoT is also a highly dynamic network due to the IoT device join, leave or failure and consequent network topology changing or failure. Heterogeneous internetworking technologies make IoT more complex and uncertain. To make IoT more trustable has many challenges but it is critical for large scale IoT deployment.

IoT is continuously collecting information about the state of the devices and circumstances. The data generated by IoT may be highly sensitive, mission critical and need to be shared with other parties, machines and services. But it also means that this data is vulnerable and open for hackers to potentially misuse. The blockchain enabled encrypted distributed ledger fits for privacy or confidentiality scenarios of IoT systems. It is a verifiable, secure, tamperproof, and permanent method of recording data by getting down the data generated by IoT into blockchain. And, the identification, configuration information of IoT can be also be retrieved from blockchain. Blockchains bring higher security level by enforcing access control, encryption that are hard to breach. Blockchain enabled encryption and distributed immutable storage means that the information recorded can be trusted by all parties involved, including machine-to-machine interactions. In an IoT where there are multiple and/or heterogeneous networks owned by multiple organizations and vendors, the oversight inside the networks and across borders can be recorded by relevant parties via blockchain. In this scenario, a permanent immutable record means custodianship, auditability, and traceability. Blockchain enables trustable IoT for both internal and external parties.

Besides, the smart contract enables authorizing distributed heterogeneous machine-to-machine interactions and task executions in a trustable way even without human involvement.

Due to the diversity of IoT, any current single blockchain cannot satisfy the demands with high efficiency and flexibility. Blockchain Federation that integrates multi-blockchain functionalities to enable trustable IoT [2].

The main contributions of this research are as follows:

- We propose a Blockchain Federation enabled trustable IoT architecture.
- We implement a proof of concept system.

- We analyze the main stream IoT architectures and discuss future research directions.

The rest of paper is organized as follows: Sect. 2 introduces the background. Section 3 presents the Blockchain Federation, the integration of different blockchains to satisfy the demands of IoT. Section 4 describes the novel Blockchain Federation based trustable IoT architecture in detail. Section 5 presents the experimental results and analysis. Section 6 summarizes the related works. Section 7 concludes the paper.

2 Background

2.1 IoT

The IoT has been defined in Recommendation ITU-T Y.2060[1] as an infrastructure enabling advanced services by interconnecting physical and virtual things based on interoperable information and communication technologies. Generally, IoT is a system of interrelated computing devices, machines, other objects and even animals or humans with automatic data transfer. There are also similar concepts such as IoE (Internet of Everything), M2M (Machine to Machine), CPS (Cyber Physical Systems), WoT (Web of Things), Wireless Sensor Network (WSN), and so on in different context. We adopt IoT in this paper to describe the common issues in the above systems.

With the rapid development of smart devices and the increase of wireless network bandwidth, the concept of the IoT is gradually being widely accepted and popularized. However, the resources of IoT devices such as the power supply, computing capacity, and storage space are limited. This makes it difficult to implement the security solutions in IoT networks, even these can be easily applied in traditional computer systems [3].

And from a broader perspective, the IoT can be perceived as a technologically and socially meaningful vision. IoT devices are functioning in many fields: personal accessories, house appliances, healthcare, smart homes, smart cities, supply chain management, manufacturing, identity management and access control, electricity market systems, insurance systems, and etc. The smart and efficient IoT systems also inspire societal innovation. For example: real time home health monitoring expands the capacity of traditional clinic/hospital, intelligent transport system reducing travel time, cost and accidents of passengers and cargo transportation.

2.2 Trustable Issues

Despite the economic and societal benefits of IoT, the trustable issues it gives rise to are obstructing the road of wider adoption. The trustable issues include security, scalability, privacy, safety, connectivity, and etc. Reliability, availability, robustness, and compliance are related with or impacted by these issues. The various types of Things in IoT incur the exchange of sensitive information taking place automatically even without the awareness of users leads to security problems. Violations of data privacy and integrity are vital for both IoT operation and rights of related individuals. When Industrial IoT involved in the energy, utilities, government, healthcare and finance sectors, the seriousness of the

---

[1] https://www.itu.int/ITU-T/recommendations/rec.aspx?rec=y.2060.

situation becomes more critical. Vulnerabilities in these systems are not only privacy violations, but also hazard of safety and availability.

According to the definition of Trusted Computing Group (TCG)[2], trust is the expectation that a device will behave in a particular manner for a specific purpose. In fact, TCG also inherits the concept of trust from Trusted Computer System Evaluation Criteria (TCSEC) and it is approximately equivalent security. The TCSEC was the first major computer security evaluation methodology. It is also known as the Orange Book because of the colorful cover, part of the Rainbow Series developed by the Department of Defense in the 1980's. It is on confidentiality and the protection of government classified information. The *trusted* is delivered from the trust in similar core concept.

The TCSEC evaluation methodology had three fundamental problems[3]:

Criteria Creep. TCSEC evaluation classes are inevitably gradual expanded. The criteria needed to be interpreted for new products.

Timeless of the Process. Too much time took in understanding of the depth of the evaluation, interactions among the evaluation teams, scheduling problems and possible misunderstandings about the evaluation practice and management.

Focused on OS. TCSEC is trying to help developers produce secure products but security issues had expanded far beyond operating systems.

Another term trustworthy is deserving of trust[4], it is from an external perspective. In this paper, Trustable is capable of being trusted to emphasize the intrinsic characteristics and also covers Scalability, Privacy, Safety, Connectivity alongside security. Creating secure hardware for the IoT is not our focal point in this paper.

The major technical challenges to overcome while marching to trustable IoT include[5,6]:

Security. Security vulnerabilities can be incurred by poorly designed devices, which can expose user data without adequate protection. Potentially malicious Things being added to IoT may provide innumerable attack vectors to carry out evil deeds that hard to be detected.

Scalability. IoT devices often lack the computational power, storage capacity and even proper software stack to be able to deploy trustable functionalities.

Privacy. Personally identifiable information leakage incurs challenges to privacy that goes beyond the data privacy issues. And, there are Things deployed in our environments without our consciousness of using.

---

[2] https://trustedcomputinggroup.org/.

[3] https://www.cs.clemson.edu/course/cpsc420/material/Evaluation/TCSEC.pdf.

[4] https://wikidiff.com/trustworthy/trustable.

[5] https://iot.ieee.org/newsletter/march-2017/three-major-challenges-facing-iot.

[6] https://www2.eecs.berkeley.edu/Pubs/TechRpts/2017/EECS-2017-234.pdf.

Safety. The physical Things are part of IoT, which allows the virtual world to interact with the physical world. e.g., The theft, changing, moving of unattended Things incurs risks to the whole IoT system.

Connectivity. Innumerable and heterogeneous Things will defy the structure of current communication models and the underlying technologies. The centralized model is sufficient for IoT anymore. Edge computing takes over mission critical operations and peer to peer communications, mesh networks take over the traffic.

2.3 Blockchain and IoT

Blockchain is built on a distributed digital ledger of transactions that is owned across all participating entities in a peer to peer network. It is widely known as an underlying technology of Bitcoin. But its scope beyond cryptocurrencies and found applications in a variety of scenarios nowadays. It is an important technology for building trustable architecture. Decentralized participating entities verify and confirm the transactions using common consensus process to reach an agreement and once verified, confirmed, and recorded, the transaction data cannot be altered anymore. Blockchain saves data blocks that are chained together to form a continuously growing list of data records. The information about every transaction is shared and available to all involved parties. Blockchain presents a decentralized solution, which does not require a third-party for achieving the trust among mutual parties, also known as trustless. Parties do not necessarily trust each other while performing transactions. This attribute makes the system more transparent than centralized transactions. Furthermore, blockchain technology provides anonymity, security, privacy, and transparency to its users. It answers the challenge of trust in a very consistent way. However, trust in IoT ecosystems goes beyond that [4]. While the data exchange aspect if pretty obvious it's certainly foremost about those untrusting constituents.

There are three major benefits of blockchain for IoT, according to IBM[7]:

Building Trust. Build trust between parties and devices, reduce risk of collusion and tampering.

Cost Reduction. Reduce costs by removing overhead associated with middlemen and intermediaries.

The Acceleration of Transactions. Reduce settlement time from days to near instantaneous.

The Things in IoT acquire information about the surrounding environment and themselves. They communicate with each other and produce large amounts of data. Furthermore, IoT suffers the constraints of such as limited energy, processing resources, and communication capacity. The deployment, maintenance, and governance are also facing challenges. IoT usually needs extra resource of computing, storage, network, and other services. It means that any current blockchain cannot satisfy all the demands simultaneously. We adopt Blockchain Federation that consolidates several blockchains to support IoT.

---

[7] https://developer.ibm.com/articles/iot-governance-01/.

3 Blockchain Federation

As discussed in previous section, a current blockchain cannot satisfy all the trustable demands of IoT. Blockchain Federation integrated two or more blockchains and necessary improvements to solve the related problems of blockchains to meet the requirements of security, scalability, privacy, safety, and connectivity to enable trustable IoT. The Blockchain Federation is a model for integrating multi-blockchain functionalities with possible performance, security, acceptability and other improvements. It enables the support of trustable IoT basing on current blockchains.

The core target of Blockchain Federation is to provide a methodology to support distributed applications that cannot be done by a single blockchain. The major targets of Blockchain Federation for IoT are:

Function Integration enriches the supporting to Things in IoT to provide blockchain services for fast network connection, more flexible data storage, and computing resource pool. Blockchain Federation enables the cooperation of independent blockchains to maximize the automation and robust of IoT.

Performance Improvement includes throughput promotion and latency reduction. For a given blockchain it is applicable to duplicate blockchain for parallel processing. The latency of a blockchain can be improved by adopting low latency network connections and more powerful computers. The side blockchain and off blockchain can improve the performance of main blockchain significantly.

The major **performance metrics** of blockchain are in the following:

Transaction Rate measures how many transactions per second are added to the memory pool of transactions awaiting confirmation. In fact, it may drastically increase or decrease from the declared rate, this can be caused by network congestion, or a major node experiencing downtime.

Storage Capacity is obvious much higher in blockchains comparing with applications only keep local copy of data. Each block will be duplicated as many times as blockchain active node number even though there are lots of nodes in blockchain network will not keep full data copy.

Consistency Delay of blockchain includes the propagation delay in the network, consensus process delay and conflict resolving delay.

The Blockchain Federation has three characteristics. The multi-blockchain connection enables the information exchanging. The inter-blockchain anchor enables the mutual proof. And, the Elasticity enables the fast Blockchain Federation deployment and resource allocation and release:

Multi-Blockchain Connection enables information exchange across blockchains.

Inter-Blockchain Anchor is to use other blockchain(s) for existence proof. It provides a way for higher level of tamper-resistant. The anchor is a hash value of a blockchain block data is written in another blockchain's block. The later blockchain proofs the existence of block data in the former one.

Elasticity means all blockchains involved in the Blockchain Federation are pluggable, i.e., Blockchain Federation can choose alternative blockchain and will not impact the implementation and operation of current blockchains. Blockchain capabilities can be elastically provisioned and released, i.e., a Blockchain Federation can be applied to a distributed application with minimal configuration effort and can be released instantly.

The Blockchain Federation includes permissionless, permissioned and hybrid deployment models:

Permissionless Model is provisioned for open access by the general public and all the blockchains involved are permissionless blockchains.

Permissioned Model is provisioned for exclusive use by an organization or interesting group with only permissioned blockchains.

Hybrid Model is a composition of permissionless and permissioned blockchains. Usually full access to any Blockchain Federation's permissioned blockchain is granted.

A permissionless model is used for public used scenarios. A permissioned model is used inside an organization. A hybrid model usually crosses the boarder of an organization.

4   Blockchain Federation Enabled IoT Architecture

IoT is a system of connected heterogeneous devices that can communicate with other devices, gather, share, and process information to deliver a certain service. e.g., some IoT devices should keep connection with the back-end if existed and be able to receive firmware upgrading when necessary; authentication and access control services to secure computing resources and networks. The internal and external hardware and software composes an ecosystem. A detailed technical reference architecture can be created to support that ecosystem and to demonstrate IoT solutions for organizations to adopt based on their specific needs.

Figure 1 depicts the IoT reference model defined in ITU-T Y.2060. It contains four layers.

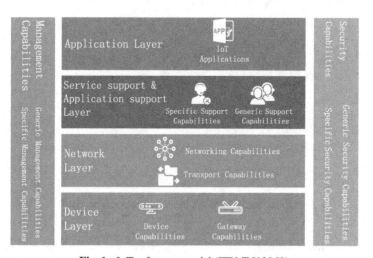

Fig. 1. IoT reference model (ITU-T Y.2060)

Application layer contains IoT applications.

Service support and application support layer consists of the following two capability groupings.

Network layer consists of the following two types of capabilities: Networking capabilities provide relevant control functions of network connectivity, such as access and transport resource control functions, mobility management or authentication, authorization and accounting (AAA). Transport capabilities focus on providing connectivity for the transport of IoT service and application specific data information, as well as the transport of IoT-related control and management information.

Device layer capabilities can be logically categorized into two kinds of capabilities: device capabilities and gateway capabilities.

Management capabilities include generic management capabilities such as device management, local network topology management, traffic and congestion management, and also specific management capabilities are closely coupled with application-specific requirements.

Figure 2 depicts a simple IoT reference architecture from IBM[8]. It consists of four layers:

Security capabilities include generic security capabilities such as authorization, authentication, application data confidentiality and integrity protection, privacy protection, security audit, anti-virus, use data, signaling data confidentiality, signaling integrity protection, device integrity validation, access control, data confidentiality and integrity protection, and specific security capabilities are closely coupled with application-specific requirements, e.g., mobile payment, security requirements.

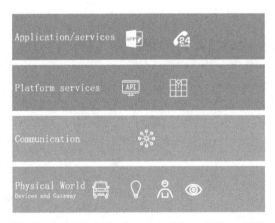

Fig. 2. A simple IoT reference architecture from IBM

Application layer manages the collection, processing, analyzing, and persisting of the large volume of sensor data in near real time. This layer supports a high data rate, which is much higher than general IT infrastructure. It also implements predictive

---

[8] https://developer.ibm.com/articles/iot-governance-01/.

analytics capabilities and addresses security, such as data security, role-based data access, and control functions.

Platform layer provides for sensor data management, application integration, and device management. This layer supports internet-scale messaging, including data collection, publish/subscribe, data mediation, data dispatching, and of course security management.

Communication layer provides a reliable network for capturing and controlling sensor data. It supports for reliably transporting data from devices to the IoT platform.

Physical devices layer supports the wide variety of sensors, devices, and gateways. It supports remote monitoring and management. This layer addresses security, such as secured booting, firmware upgrading, intrusion detection, and logging of security events.

Table 1. Classes of constrained devices (KiB = 1024 bytes).

Name	Data size (e.g., RAM)	Code size (e.g., Flash)
Class 0, C0	≪10 KiB	≪100 KiB
Class 1, C1	˜10 KiB	˜100 KiB
Class 2, C2	˜10 KiB	˜250 KiB

However, IoT devices have heterogeneous capabilities in terms of processing power, storage capacity, and energy supply. Therefore, there are constrained devices with limit RAM and Flash. Table 1 gives the classes of constrained devices according to RFC7228[9]. And to support complex applications and business logic, more layers introduced to fit more functionalities. Internet of Things World Forum[10] gives a seven layer IoT reference model depicted in Fig. 3.

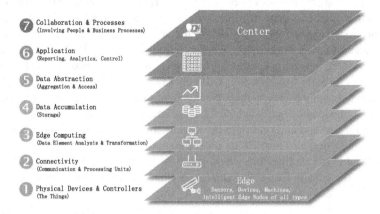

Fig. 3. Internet of Things world forum IoT reference model

---

[9] https://tools.ietf.org/html/rfc7228.

[10] https://blogs.cisco.com/news/the-internet-of-things-moving-beyond-the-hype.

Gartner IoT Reference Model[11] is described in Fig. 4. It provides a more complex reference model with tiers (Edge Tier, Platform Tier and Enterprise Tier), layers (Device layer, Communication layer, Information layer, function layer and Process layer), interfaces (Layer Interfaces and Tier Interfaces) and security model. But, the trustable modules or functionalities are absent.

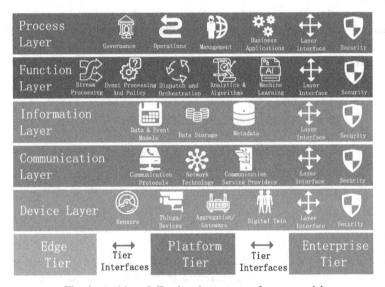

Fig. 4. Architect IoT using the gartner reference model

As discussed in Sect. 2 and 3, current IoT reference models adopt security technologies to enable the so-called trusted or trustworthy IoT system. In fact, the intrinsic trustable features are absent from all these models. In Sect. 3 we reviewed the Blockchain Federation that optimizes the performance of blockchains and fit for different and complex application scenarios. We simplify the hierarchy of IoT to four layers according to the advance of devices nowadays. We also introduce AI, Big Data with Blockchain Federation as three tiers to meet other higher level requirements. Blockchain Federation is the core tier to build trustable IoT. Different layer may adopt different blockchain. And, current AI technologies such as face recognition, object detection are also integrated with embedded devices such as CCTV camera and so on. In each layer of IoT data collection, storage and real time processing are also performing simultaneously. We assign Big Data tier to host all the related components. The Blockchain Federation enabled trustable IoT architecture we proposed is depicted in Fig. 5. It is an Artificial Intelligence, Blockchain, Cloud, Big Data, Everything, and Fog Computing (ABCDEF) integrated IoT reference architecture.

---

[11] www.gartner.com.

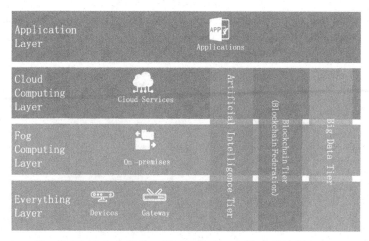

Fig. 5. Blockchain Federation enabled trustable IoT architecture

5 Example Case Study

5.1 Proof of Concept IoT System

We setup an Ultra Wide Band (UWB) based location system as proof of concept IoT following the Blockchain Federation enabled trustable IoT architecture in Fig. 5 proposed in Sect. 4. The major hardware components include anchors, tags, gateways and edge computing devices in Fig. 6. Two cloud servers provided by Aliyun[12] are setup as database server. The IoT system performs blockchain based location and position information collection using distributed ledger. And, the firmware upgrading uses another distributed ledger cooperated with bandwidth sharing blockchain for verification and file transferring.

The following are the detailed configuration of the devices and applications.

Anchor/tag
Hardware: DWM1001/Bluetooth/CR123 battery
Software: eCos RTOS

Gateway
Hardware: Raspberry Pi 3B/1G RAM
Software: Linux Kernel Module, Gateway Daemon, Gateway Proxy, MQTT Broker and Web Manager

Fog Computing Device
Hardware: Intel ATOM x5-Z8350/4G RAM/32G eMMC
Software: Ubuntu 18.04, MySQL 8.0.11

We setup NKN[13] blockchain nodes as the peer to peer sensitive data transportation on the fog computing device. Hyperledger[14] is used as the data integration service on

---

[12] www.aliyun.com.
[13] www.nkn.org.
[14] www.hyperledger.org.

cloud server and fog computing device. One NKN and two Hyperledger blockchains are combined together as Blockchain Federation.

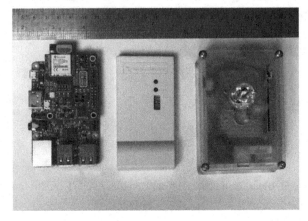

Fig. 6. Gateway, anchor/tag, fog computing device (from left to right)

5.2   Test Cases

The following are the detailed test cases and results.

Case 1: Location is used to verify the IoT system works well. Figure 7 is the screenshot of Android App depicts the location result and anchor/tag status. All the data will be verified by peers via Hyperledger.

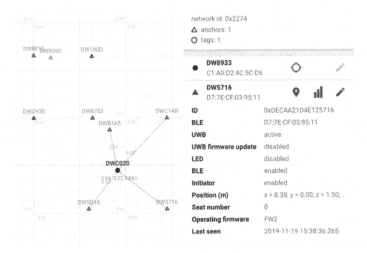

Fig. 7. Location result and anchor/tag status

Case 2: Firmware upgrading is used to verify the IoT system with Blockchain Federation is trustable for unattended upgrading. Figure 8 is the screenshot of the result. All the tags received correct firmware version through NKN blockchain and verified through the distributed ledger.

Fig. 8. Unattended firmware upgrading

Case 3: Cloud based trustable IoT data collection is used to verify the IoT system with Blockchain Federation is trustable with tamperproof data collection. Figure 9 shows the statistical result of record number and latest update timestamp transmitted via Hyperledger.

Fig. 9. Cloud based trustable IoT data collection

The test cases show that our proof of concept system works well and also reflect the correctness and feasibility of the proposed reference architecture.

6 Related Work

The trustable issues include security, scalability, privacy, safety, connectivity and so on. Many researches focus on specific directions. Ouaddah [5] introduced a decentralized authorization management framework using blockchain. It uses new types of transactions to grant or revoke access for users. Novo [6] proposed a fully distributed access control scheme for IoT systems based on blockchain. Angin [7] introduces transparency and tamperproof into data storage and retrieval in IoT networks. Sigwart [8] identified requirements for a generic IoT data provenance framework, and conceptualise the framework as a layered architecture. Ali [9] proposed a decentralized access model for IoT data, using a a modular consortium architecture for IoT and blockchains. Buccafurri [10] proposed protocol leverages the popular social network Twitter and works by building a meshed chain of tweets to ensure transaction security. Fakhri [11] proofed that the IoT system based on blockchain technology has a higher level of security than the IoT system without blockchain technology. Sharma [12] provided a secure distributed fog node architecture that uses SDN and blockchain techniques. Fog nodes are distributed fog computing entities that allow the deployment of fog services at the edge of the IoT network. Liang [13] proposed a secure Fabric blockchain-based data transmission technique for industrial IoT. This technique uses the blockchain-based dynamic secret sharing mechanism. Lv [14] proposed a privacy-preserving publish/subscribe model by using the blockchain technique, which evades the centralized trustroot setting and the problem of single point failure. Son [15] Using IPFS can ensure the integrity of the firmware. Angin [16] proposed a blockchain-based approach for IoT systems that introduces transparency and tamper-resistance into data storage and retrieval in IoT networks. Kumar [17] elaborates the related issues considering the interaction in IoT and studies how the distributed ledger contribute to it.

7 Conclusions

In this paper, we have analyzed the trust issues that impacts the design, maintenance, and governance of IoT. We clarify the concept of trustable IoT as is capable to be trusted. The trustable issues include security, scalability, privacy, safety, connectivity and so on. Due to the complexity of IoT system any current blockchain cannot satisfy all demands of heterogeneous devices, networks, and higher level functionalities. we proposed a novel Blockchain Federation based trustable IoT architecture. This architecture combines several blockchains to support heterogeneous devices and dynamic networks. The reference architecture has four layers and three tiers that clarifies the concept confusion of other layer only architectures. The UWB based Proof of Concept IoT system demonstrates the correctness and feasibility of the architecture. We also addressed the possibility of the integration of AI, Blockchain, Cloud Computing, Big Data, IoT, and Fog Computing. The AI and Big Data could be closely connected with blockchain to construct more intelligent and trustable IoT systems.

References

1. Hassija, V., Chamola, V., Saxena, V., Jain, D., Goyal, P., Sikdar, B.: A survey on IoT security: application areas, security threats, and solution architectures. IEEE Access **7**, 82721–82743 (2019). https://doi.org/10.1109/ACCESS.2019.2924045
2. Wan, Z., Cai, M., Lin, X., Yang, J.: Blockchain federation for complex distributed applications. In: Joshi, J., Nepal, S., Zhang, Q., Zhang, L.-J. (eds.) ICBC 2019. LNCS, vol. 11521, pp. 112–125. Springer, Cham (2019). https://doi.org/10.1007/978-3-030-23404-1_8
3. Tan, B., Yan, J., Chen, S., Liu, X.: The impact of blockchain on food supply chain: the case of Walmart. In: Qiu, M. (ed.) SmartBlock 2018. LNCS, vol. 11373, pp. 167–177. Springer, Cham (2018). https://doi.org/10.1007/978-3-030-05764-0_18
4. Ferrag, M.A., Derdour, M., Mukherjee, M., Derhab, A., Maglaras, L., Janicke, H.: Blockchain technologies for the Internet of Things: research issues and challenges. IEEE IoT J. **6**, 2188–2204 (2019). https://doi.org/10.1109/JIOT.2018.2882794
5. Ouaddah, A., El Kalam, A.A., Ouahman, A.A.: FairAccess: a new blockchain-based access control framework for the Internet of Things. Secur. Commun. Networks. **9**, 5943–5964 (2016). https://doi.org/10.1002/sec.1748
6. Novo, O.: Blockchain meets IoT: an architecture for scalable access management in IoT. IEEE IoT J. **5**, 1184–1195 (2018). https://doi.org/10.1109/JIOT.2018.2812239
7. Angin, P., Mert, M.B., Mete, O., Ramazanli, A., Sarica, K., Gungoren, B.: A blockchain-based decentralized security architecture for IoT. In: Georgakopoulos, D., Zhang, L.-J. (eds.) ICIOT 2018. LNCS, vol. 10972, pp. 3–18. Springer, Cham (2018). https://doi.org/10.1007/978-3-319-94370-1_1
8. Sigwart, M., Borkowski, M., Peise, M., Schulte, S., Tai, S.: Blockchain-based data provenance for the Internet of Things. In: ACM International Conference Proceeding Services (2019). https://doi.org/10.1145/3365871.3365886
9. Ali, M.S., Dolui, K., Antonelli, F.: IoT data privacy via blockchains and IPFS. In: ACM International Conference Proceeding Services (2017). https://doi.org/10.1145/3131542.313 1563
10. Buccafurri, F., Lax, G., Nicolazzo, S., Nocera, A.: Overcoming limits of blockchain for IoT applications. In: ACM International Conference Proceeding Services, Part F1305 (2017). https://doi.org/10.1145/3098954.3098983
11. Fakhri, D., Mutijarsa, K.: Secure IoT Communication using blockchain technology. In: ISESD 2018 - International Symposium on Electronic Smart Devices Smart Devices Big Data Analysis and Machine Learning, pp. 1–6 (2019). https://doi.org/10.1109/ISESD.2018. 8605485
12. Sharma, P.K., Chen, M.Y., Park, J.H.: A software defined fog node based distributed blockchain cloud architecture for IoT. IEEE Access **6**, 115–124 (2018). https://doi.org/10. 1109/ACCESS.2017.2757955
13. Liang, W., Tang, M., Long, J., Peng, X., Xu, J., Li, K.C.: A secure FaBric blockchain-based data transmission technique for industrial Internet-of-Things. IEEE Trans. Ind. Inform. **15**, 3582–3592 (2019). https://doi.org/10.1109/TII.2019.2907092
14. Lv, P., Wang, L., Zhu, H., Deng, W., Gu, L.: An IOT-oriented privacy-preserving publish/subscribe model over blockchains. IEEE Access **7**, 41309–41314 (2019). https://doi. org/10.1109/ACCESS.2019.2907599
15. Son, M., Kim, H.: Blockchain-based secure firmware management system in IoT environment. In: International Conference on Advanced Communication Technology (ICACT 2019), February, pp. 142–146 (2019). https://doi.org/10.23919/ICACT.2019.8701959

16. Bugeja, J., Jacobsson, A., Davidsson, P.: An Empirical Analysis of Smart Connected Home Data. In: Georgakopoulos, D., Zhang, L.-J. (eds.) ICIOT 2018. LNCS, vol. 10972, pp. 134–149. Springer, Cham (2018). https://doi.org/10.1007/978-3-319-94370-1_10
17. Kumar, N.M., Mallick, P.K.: Blockchain technology for security issues and challenges in IoT. Procedia Comput. Sci. **132**, 1815–1823 (2018). https://doi.org/10.1016/j.procs.2018.05.140

Decision Support for Patient Discharge in Hospitals – Analyzing the Relationship Between Length of Stay and Readmission Risk, Cost, and Profit

Isabella Eigner[✉] and Freimut Bodendorf

FAU Erlangen-Nürnberg, Lange Gasse 20, 90489 Nuremberg, Germany
isabella.eigner@fau.de

Abstract. Determining the optimal time for patient discharge is a challenging and complex task that involves multiple opposing decision perspectives. On the one hand, patient safety and the quality of healthcare service delivery and on the other hand, economic factors and resource availability need to be considered by hospital personnel. By using state-of-the-art machine learning methods, this paper presents a novel approach to determine the optimal time of patient discharge from different viewpoints, including a cost-centered, an outcome-centered, and a balanced perspective. The proposed approach has been developed and tested as part of a case study in an Australian private hospital group. For this purpose, unplanned readmissions and associated costs for episodes of admitted patient care are analyzed with regards to the respective time of discharge. The results of the analyses show that increasing the length of stay for certain procedure groups can lead to reduced costs. The developed approach can aid physicians and hospital management to make more evidence-based decisions to ensure both sufficient healthcare quality and cost-effective resource allocation in hospitals.

Keywords: Machine learning · Length of stay · Unplanned readmissions · Patient discharge

1 Introduction

The increasing demand for healthcare services as well as the change from a fee-for-service to a prospective payment system in many countries force hospitals to increase their case rate and reduce hospital length of stay (LOS) for patients. According to these payment systems, patients are classified into so-called Diagnosis-Related Groups (DRG). These groups provide a clinically meaningful way of relating a hospital's casemix to its resources, where patients with similar clinical conditions requiring comparable hospital resources are categorized into groups and priced accordingly (Fetter *et al.* 1980). This means, that hospitals are reimbursed for a patient episode with a fixed amount of money that is defined for the specific DRG independent from the duration of the patient stay. Only if the LOS exceeds or falls below the average boundaries for this DRG

© Springer Nature Switzerland AG 2020
J. E. Ferreira et al. (Eds.): SERVICES 2020, LNCS 12411, pp. 77–84, 2020.
https://doi.org/10.1007/978-3-030-59595-1_6

(i.e., so-called "low outliers" or "high outliers"), hospital reimbursement is adjusted. Thus, hospitals are motivated to shorten LOS and release patients as close to this lower boundary as possible. Studies show, that this reduction can result in higher unplanned readmission rates (Oh *et al.* 2017) that can, in turn, lead to penalty fees or reduced compensation for hospitals. Several initiatives have been introduced worldwide to tackle the issue of preventable readmissions. Most prominent are the Hospital Readmission Reduction Program (HRRP) in the US (CMS 2016) and the Australian National Healthcare Agreement for Unplanned Hospital Readmission Rates (AIHW 2018). These programs aim at identifying, monitoring, and reducing hospital readmissions according to different criteria. The starting point of these interventions lies in the screening of individuals at high risk of discharge failure (Scott 2010). By identifying high-risk patients, hospital resources can be allocated accordingly and interventions and discharge planning can be adapted. Multiple factors associated with a higher risk of readmission have been identified in research, including health factors (e.g., co-morbidities (van Walraven *et al.* 2011; Kumar *et al.* 2017)), social factors (e.g., marital status (Hasan *et al.* 2010)), clinical factors (e.g., hospital utilization (Shadmi *et al.* 2015), length of stay (Heggestad 2002)), or effective discharge management (Ohta *et al.* 2016). While some of these influences cannot be directly controlled, especially the time and management of patient discharge is a modifiable factor. While some studies suggest a longer LOS to be beneficial (Horney *et al.* 2017), others state the importance of an early release (Morris *et al.* 2011; Hasan *et al.* 2010) to avoid hospital-related issues such as infections or bed sores. While the impact of an increased LOS on the quality of healthcare services and thus, the readmission risk is still debated, the resulting costs for a prolonged stay are apparent. With each additional day of hospitalization, incurred costs for accommodation, personnel, as well as opportunity costs for the occupied hospital bed, continuously increase. These opposing views result in a complex optimization problem of finding a suitable time for patient discharge that leads to both the maximum profit for the hospital while also reducing the rate of unplanned readmissions. Therefore, the main goal of this paper is to investigate the relationship between patient LOS and readmission risks and the respective costs that need to be considered in this context and provide recommendations on determining the optimal time for patient discharge based on these factors. For this purpose, episode data from an Australian private hospital group is utilized to estimate the readmission risk for individual patients across multiple DRGs. The remainder of this paper is structured as follows: Sect. 2 gives an overview of the theoretical and conceptual foundations that are required to calculate the respective costs and outcome measures for a patient episode. Section 3 subsequently aggregates these findings into three different perspectives on the optimal time of patient discharge, namely from a solely cost-centered view, an outcome-centered view, and a balanced view. Finally, the conceptual views are tested with actual episode data and critically reflected to identify limitations and future research potentials of this work.

2 Theoretical and Conceptual Foundations

2.1 Objective and Method

Since 2006, the Australian Institute of Health and Welfare has been tracking 28-day readmission rates (AIHW 2018). Here, readmission is defined as follows:

- The second admission has to follow a separation from the same hospital where the patient was either treated with a knee replacement (TKA), hip replacement (THA), tonsillectomy and adenoidectomy (TONADE), hysterectomy (HYS), prostatectomy (PRO), cataract surgery (CAT) or appendectomy (APP).
- The second admission has to occur within 28 days of the previous separation.
- The principal diagnosis of the second admission has to refer to a complication, sequelae of complications, or post-procedural disorders from the index admission.

As readmission rates are already widely used as a measure to indicate how well a patient is taken care of (Benbassat and Taragin 2000), the readmission risk curve is implemented to showcase the impact of the discharge decision and LOS on the quality of care. In addition, economic factors, such as hospital costs and reimbursements are contrasted against this measure to disclose the impact on both perspectives to the decision-maker. Thus, doctors can determine the optimal time of patient discharge both from an economical perspective as well as according to the patient status. From an economical perspective, the lower boundary for patient length of stay is deemed optimal due to the unvarying reimbursement rates (cf. Fig. 1(a)). However, considering the risk of readmission (cf. Fig. 1(b)), a longer LOS can be preferable, depending on the underlying strategy with regards to cost efficiency and quality of care. To be able to visualize the risk of readmission for an individual patient over time as well as the respective costs and reimbursements for a single episode, several measures need to be calculated beforehand.

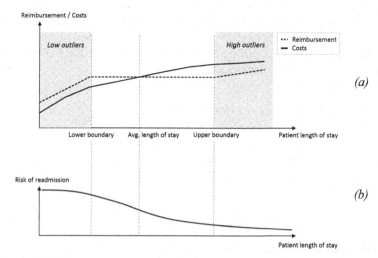

Fig. 1. Reimbursement, costs, and readmission risk for a patient episode over time

2.2 Readmission Risk Chart

To determine the readmission risk of a patient during his/her stay, historical patient episode data is utilized to develop prediction models for each of the AIHW procedure groups (Eigner *et al.* 2017; Eigner *et al.* 2018). Based on the predicted probability of readmission, the current risk is determined for the investigated episode. Thus, by understanding this risk in more detail, physicians and hospital personnel can make better-informed, more evidence-based decisions on patient discharge and additional treatment.

To realize this in practice, the most suitable prediction model is selected according to the presented diagnosis and the main performed procedure. This ensures that procedure-specific risk factors are considered in the readmission risk prediction, resulting in a higher prediction accuracy (Eigner and Cooney 2019). The model is applied to simulate the readmission risk when discharging the patient at the current point in time (i.e., for the current length of stay) as well as the following days with an increasing length of stay. This results in a readmission risk curve that determines the risk progression over time to indicate the optimal time of discharge from a quality point-of-view.

2.3 Cost Chart

To determine the cost development over time, the National Hospital Cost Data Collection (NHCDC) Australian Public Hospitals Cost Report is used to calculate the average costs per DRG (IHPA 2018). Here, costs are categorized according to various cost buckets that reflect certain cost pools within a hospital. Each bucket summarizes the costs for a particular function in a hospital (e.g., the operating room). Overall, sixteen cost buckets are differentiated. While certain buckets, for example, prosthesis and imaging, are assumed to be independent of the actual LOS and therefore constant for a certain procedure group, hotel costs continuously grow with an increased LOS. Following the approach by Arefian *et al.* (2016), costs of accommodation, medical treatment, laboratory procedures, materials and services, and physician and nursing care are included in the cost per bed day calculation. On-costs, operating room, prosthesis, depreciation and imaging costs are aggregated as procedure-specific costs that are independent of the LOS. Table 1 provides the average costs for each procedure group, including the LOS-independent procedure costs and the LOS-dependent costs per bed day.

Table 1. Average costs for each AIHW procedure group (in $)

	APP	CAT	HYS	PRO	THA	TKA	TONADE
Procedure costs	4,652	2,696	8,067	4,446	16,217	16,033	2,136
Cost per bed day	1,384	1,253	1,617	1,398	1,359	1,396	1,566

2.4 Reimbursement Chart

To calculate the reimbursement rate for each episode, the Victorian Weighted Inlier Equivalent Separation (WIES) is used. Episodes with a shorter or longer length of stay compared to an average range ("inliers") for each DRG are reimbursed according to different pre-defined weights. Each WIES is multiplied by a base price (b), namely the Australian National Efficient Price (NEP). For 2018–19, the NEP is valued at \$ 5,012 (IHPA 2018). Inlier episodes with a LOS over one day use the standard multi-day inlier weight for that DRG. For a shorter hospital LOS, a low outlier per diem cost weight is used as a basis for reimbursement calculation. An extended LOS uses a high outlier per diem weight.

Additional weights are applied for one-day or same-day stays and hospital-in-the-home days as well as cost weights for co-payments to moderate financial risk for hospitals that provide special types of care (DHHS 2018). The WIES cost weight for same-day episodes, one-day episodes, and multi-day inliers are available directly in the WIES25 weights table (DHHS 2018). As reimbursement is determined based on the episode's DRG, which is assigned only post-admission, the most likely DRG must be identified in advance. To determine the DRG pre-discharge, a logistic regression model is applied. Based on the suggested DRG, the responding WIES weights are utilized to display the final reimbursement rate.

3   Optimal Time of Patient Discharge

To determine the optimal time of patient discharge, the presented measures are used to develop three perspectives from a profit-centered, a quality-centered and a balanced viewpoint. For the profit-centered perspective, only costs and reimbursements are considered to identify the most financially rewarding time for patient discharge. Figure 2 displays the recommendation for an average patient after a knee replacement with major complexity to discharge on the second day for a maximum profit.

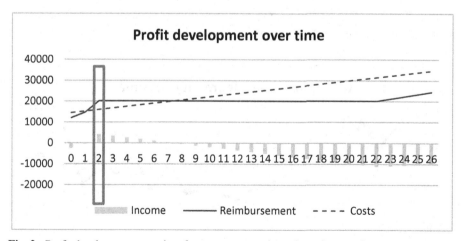

Fig. 2. Profit development over time for an average patient after a knee replacement with major complexity (DRG I04A)

The second perspective is based on the prospective readmission risk during the hospital stay. Figure 3 displays the average proportion of patients that were readmitted in the past according to their time of discharge. From a healthcare quality perspective, the ninth day is selected to be the optimal point of discharge with the lowest readmission risk. While this visualization only considers the length of stay as the influencing factor for readmission risk, the developed prediction models include additional risk factors specific to each procedure group. The increasing risk depicted in Fig. 3 is mainly due to the occurrence of complex cases with multiple complications. For episodes without any major incidents, an increased length of stay is associated with a higher quality of care and thus a reduced risk of readmission (cf. Fig. 1). However, as patients are usually released once they're sufficiently healed, this is not directly reflected in the historical data.

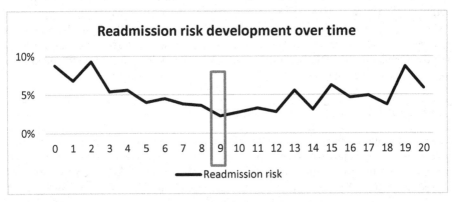

Fig. 3. Proportion of readmissions for patients after a knee replacement (DRG I04A)

To combine both perspectives into a balanced view that considers both economical as well as quality measures, both measures are combined into one visualization (Fig. 4).

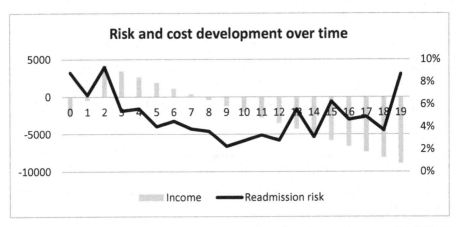

Fig. 4. Risk and cost development for an average patient after a knee replacement (DRG I04A)

To quantify the readmission risk to allow for better comparability, this measure can also be transformed into a cost factor. This is done by multiplying the current readmission risk with the average cost for a readmission episode. However, this approach neglects reputation damages.

4 Discussion and Conclusion

The increasing pressure on healthcare professionals to deliver high-quality patient care with restricted time and resources is forcing hospitals to find more efficient ways of providing healthcare services. To counter this issue, this paper presents a concept to support hospital personnel to consider both the economical as well as the quality-driven viewpoint in the patient discharge decision by analyzing previous patient episodes. The implications of this study are relevant to both research and practice. Considering the quality of care and regulatory penalties, the importance of identifying patients at high risk of readmission is apparent. Improved post-discharge care and support for self-care can help to abate potential readmissions of identified individuals, thereby reducing overall costs and increasing healthcare quality (Shulan *et al.* 2013). Thus, by aiding the identification of potential risk patients, hospital resources can be better allocated to critical patients, and health interventions are already possible in an early stage of the patient pathway.

References

AIHW: National Healthcare Agreement: PI 23–Unplanned hospital readmission rates, 2018 (2018). https://meteor.aihw.gov.au/content/index.phtml/itemId/658485

Arefian, H., et al.: Extra length of stay and costs because of health care-associated infections at a German university hospital. Am. J. Infection Control **44**(2), 160–166 (2016)

Benbassat, J., Taragin, M.: Hospital readmissions as a measure of quality of health care. Arch. Intern. Med. **160**(8), 1074 (2000)

CMS: Readmissions Reduction Program (HRRP) (2016). https://www.cms.gov/medicare/medicare-fee-for-service-payment/acuteinpatientpps/readmissions-reduction-program.html

DHHS: WIES25 weights 2018–19 (2018). https://www2.health.vic.gov.au/about/publications/FormsAndTemplates/wies-swies-calculator-2018-19

Eigner, I., Cooney, A.: A literature review on predicting unplanned patient readmissions. In: Wickramasinghe, N., Bodendorf, F. (eds.) Delivering Superior Health and Wellness Management with IoT and Analytics. HDIA, pp. 259–282. Springer, Cham (2019). https://doi.org/10.1007/978-3-030-17347-0_12

Eigner, I., Reischl, D., Bodendorf, F.: Development and evaluation of ensemble-based classification models for predicting unplanned hospital readmissions after hysterectomy. In: ACIS 2018 Proceedings (2018)

Eigner, I., Tajak, L., Bodendorf, F., Wickramasinghe, N.: Readmission risk prediction for patients after total hip or knee arthroplasty. In: ACIS 2017 Proceedings (2017)

Fetter, R.B., Shin, Y., Freeman, J.L., Averill, R.F., Thompson, J.D.: Case mix definition by diagnosis-related groups. Med. Care **18**(2), Suppl. iii, 1–53 (1980)

Hasan, O., et al.: Hospital readmission in general medicine patients: a prediction model. J. Gen. Intern. Med. **25**(3), 211–219 (2010)

Heggestad, T.: Do hospital length of stay and staffing ratio affect elderly patients' risk of readmission? A nation-wide study of norwegian hospitals. Health Serv. Res. **37**(3), 647–665 (2002)

Horney, C., Capp, R., Boxer, R., Burke, R.E.: Factors associated with early readmission among patients discharged to post-acute care facilities. J. Am. Geriatr. Soc. **65**(6), 1199–1205 (2017)

IHPA: HPA releases National Efficient Price and National Efficient Cost Determinations (2018). https://www.ihpa.gov.au/media-releases/ihpa-releases-national-efficient-price-and-national-efficient-cost-determinations

Kumar, A., et al.: Comorbidity indices versus function as potential predictors of 30-day readmission in older patients following postacute rehabilitation. J. Gerontol. Ser. A Biol. Sci. Med. Sci. **72**(2), 223–228 (2017)

Morris, D.S., et al.: The surgical revolving door: risk factors for hospital readmission. J. Surg. Res. **170**(2), 297–301 (2011)

Oh, J.-H.C., Zheng, Z.E., Bardhan, I.R.: Sooner or later? Health information technology, length of stay and readmission risk. Prod. Oper. Manag. **27**(11), 2038–2053 (2017)

Ohta, B., Mola, A., Rosenfeld, P., Ford, S.: Early discharge planning and improved care transitions: pre-admission assessment for readmission risk in an elective orthopedic and cardiovascular surgical population. Int. J. Integr. Care **16**(2), 10 (2016)

Scott, I.A.: Preventing the rebound: improving care transition in hospital discharge processes. Aust. Health Rev. **34**(4), 445–451 (2010)

Shadmi, E., Flaks-Manov, N., Hoshen, M., Goldman, O., Bitterman, H., Balicer, R.D.: Predicting 30-day readmissions with preadmission electronic health record data. Med. Care **53**(3), 283–289 (2015)

Shulan, M., Gao, K., Moore, C.D.: Predicting 30-day all-cause hospital readmissions. Health Care Manag. Sci. **16**(2), 167–175 (2013)

van Walraven, C., Bennett, C., Jennings, A., Austin, P.C., Forster, A.J.: Proportion of hospital readmissions deemed avoidable: a systematic review. CMAJ **183**(7), E391–E402 (2011)

AIServiceX: A Knowledge Graph-Based Intelligent Question-Answering System for Personal Services

Yao Sun[1,2], Wenming Gui[1], Cheng Han[3], Yan Zhang[1], and Shudong Zhang[4(✉)]

[1] School of Software Engineering, Jinling Institute of Technology, Nanjing 211169, China
`{suny216,gwm,zy}@jit.edu.cn`
[2] Nanjing Institute of Big Data, Jinling Institute of Technology, Nanjing 211169, China
[3] School of Computer Engineering, Jinling Institute of Technology, Nanjing 211169, China
`hc@jit.edu.cn`
[4] Information Engineering College, Capital Normal University, Beijing 100048, China
`zsd@cnu.edu.cn`

Abstract. Knowledge graph-based question-answering systems are widely used in e-commerce enterprises. They can reduce the costs of customer services and improve service capabilities. The description of questions is often ambiguous, and the knowledge graph's update in online personal services always has a high overhead. To address the above issues, by augmenting domain semantics, this paper proposes a knowledge graph-based intelligent question-answering system called as AIServiceX. It employs a gate recurrent unit model to identify entities and assertions, and then gets the most related semantic augmentation contents from existing external domain knowledge via topic comparison. Then, it ranks all the candidates to get optimal answers by discovering several heuristic rules. Periodically, it augments the global knowledge graph with minimized updating costs with an Integer linear programming resolving model. This mechanism can recognize question entities precisely, and map domain knowledge to the KG automatically, which achieves a high answering precision with a low overhead. Experiments with a production e-commerce data show that AIServiceX can improve the precision.

Keywords: Knowledge graph · Question-Answering system · Gate recurrent unit · Personal services

1 Introduction

Knowledge graph (KG) is one of key technologies for implementing an intelligent question and answer service (QA), which can reduce customers' service costs and improve their self-service capabilities. Although the current methods based on natural language processing can well deal with the problems of context semantics and language fuzziness, the existing QA services based on KG is still far from industrial applications. Firstly, current methods retrieve information with neural network and dialogue model to improve the efficiency of constructing KGs, but they cannot well utilize and merge knowledge in

© Springer Nature Switzerland AG 2020
J. E. Ferreira et al. (Eds.): SERVICES 2020, LNCS 12411, pp. 85–92, 2020.
https://doi.org/10.1007/978-3-030-59595-1_7

different domains. Furthermore, current methods deal with the shortage knowledge in KG by means of context semantic association [1], web page search [2] and external text [3], but the lack of external knowledge and the automatic integration of KGs lead to a high cost of·operating and managing online services and cannot well satisfy customers' requirements.

To address the above issues, this paper proposes a Knowledge graph-based intelligent question-answering service AIServiceX. Firstly, we propose an entity/assertion recognition method based on a gate recurrent unit (GRU) model combined with the attention model and the dual-phase connection to achieve the accurate recognition of natural language's expression. Secondly, we propose a semantic enhancement method based on the topic comparison, which considers the loss of two squares and a topic model, and thus the domain knowledge mapped to a local KG supports the online update of a knowledge base. Meanwhile, we employ heuristic query rules to sort the candidate set by combining questions' features and KG's status, so that we can easily select the best candidate answers. Finally, we employ the optimization strategy based on the integer linear programming (ILP) to update the local KG according to the users' satisfaction and services' cost. The GRU model and semantic enhancement method can realize the construction and expansion of KG and have the flexible online service capability. Heuristic rules and the ILP optimization strategy can support the retrieval and update of KG in AIServiceX and ensure its availability.

2 Methodology

We take questions expressed in Chinese language as input and the answers of matched questions expressed in the KG as output. AIServiceX receiving requests to answer questions includes six phases as follows.

Question input (Phase 1). AIServiceX receives users' questions from different interfaces, and then transmits these questions to Phase 2 with identity authentication. Different users may have different expressions for similar questions in the input. Each user has his own question intentions or expected answers, so the forwarded questions is uncertain and fuzzy;

GRU identification (Phase 2). AIServiceX receives questions forwarded by Phase 1, and then identifies the entities/assertions from the received texts via word segmentation, which are the query condition of Phase 3. AIServiceX overcomes the fuzziness of Phase 1 through the GRU's dual-phase connection and attention weight. Thus, AIServiceX outputs more accurate recognition results described as a target vector reflecting users' main attention;

Tendency analysis (Phase 3). AIServiceX takes the entity/assertion vector identified in Phase 2 as input, queries keywords from different knowledge bases to find all relevant texts of the questions, and then takes the text with the highest matching degree as input of the next phase. AIServiceX takes historical data of various knowledge bases to construct a tendency analysis model based on a topic model, and then outputs the best matched text through combining the maximum likelihood estimation and the least square loss;

KG enhancement (Phase 4). AIServiceX enhances the original KG by adding edges and points to construct an enhanced KG based query database. This phase integrates the KG and external texts to automatically update KG for online service, and thus continuously improves the knowledge quantity and the expression ability of KG;

Heuristic query (Phase 5). AIServiceX queries KG to obtain an answer candidate set ac-cording to the entity/assertion vectors of the updated global KG from Phase 4, sorts the answers by the counting historical accesses, provides the answers with the highest score, and then records the status of this questioning and answering process. The heuristic rules consider the questions and the overall status of KG;

Periodic update (Phase 6). AIServiceX periodically pulls and normalizes the status of all questions in Phase 5, and quantifies the response time and users' satisfaction with the integer linear programming model to achieve the minimum of the KG update cost.

3 Algorithm

According to the above methodology, Table 1 describes the algorithm of answering questions in detail as follows. AIServiceX trains the GRU model for each entity to minimize the entity identification loss (lines 1–5); trains the GRU model for each assertion to minimize the assertion identification loss (lines 6–10); gets entities and assertions from the trained GRU model's outputs according to input questions (line 11); queries knowledge bases with the above output to obtain enhanced text of each knowledge base (line 12); employs the topic model and the quadratic loss to find the most similar text, and then constructs the local KG (lines 13–17); uses heuristic rules to sort answer candidate sets (lines 18–23); regularly updates the global KG (lines 24–33); initializes ILP's input (lines 25–29); performs ILP solution and merges local KGs according to the results (lines 30–33).

Table 1. The algorithm of answering questions.

Input: a question set q;
Output: the answer of q: a_q

1.	$L = \text{splitWords}(q)$
2.	$\text{setInputs}(q)$
3.	while $\|\hat{p}_\ell - \frac{1}{L}\sum_{j=1}^{L} r_j^T\|_2 > loss_p$
4.	Update $(\{W\}, w, \{b\}, b_q)$
5.	end for
6.	$L = \text{splitWords}(q)$
7.	$\text{setInputs}(L \text{ tokens in } q, h \text{ of } q)$
8.	while $\|e_h - \frac{1}{L}\sum_{j=1}^{L} r_j^T\|_2 > loss_e$
9.	Update $(matrics, bias)$
10.	end for
11.	In predicate learning model, $input(q) \rightarrow \hat{p}_\ell$
12.	In head entity learning model, $input(q) \rightarrow \hat{e}_h$
13.	In augment texts: $query\langle\hat{p}_\ell, \hat{e}_h\rangle \rightarrow \{text_i\}$
14.	for $text_i$ in $\{text_i\}$

(continued)

Table 1. (*continued*)

15. $L'_{rp\text{-}max} = \text{findMax}(L'_{rp-i})$
16.   end for
17.   buildlocalKG(L'_{rp-max},text$_{max}$)
18.   for C_i in {candidiate$_i$}
19.   setCounts(candidate$_i$)
20.   setCosSimilarity(Q_i,A_j,C_i)
21.   end for
22.   quickSort({candidiate$_i$},{similarity$_i$},{counts$_i$})
23.   set a to compact (C_0)
24.   In a *period*:
25.   for QA$_i$ in QA$_g$ do
26.   setTime (QA$_i$. *timeSet*)
27.   setUs(QA$_i$.uS)
28.   ILPInput(QA$_i$)
29.   end for
30.   ILPResolver({QA$_i$})
31.   Update({QA$_i$},uD$_i$ == 1)
32.   increment(point$_i$)
33.   end for

---

4 Design

Figure 1 shows the service architecture of AIServiceX including an entrance layer, a resource access layer, a KG service layer and a knowledge base layer.

Entrance layer. AIServiceX and other applications share the same traffic entry with a unified LDAP authentication for permission. Thus, AIServiceX can implement the integrated management for multiple services to avoid confusion in resource utilization and security issues;

KG service layer. AIServiceX implements key technologies in a microservice architecture (i.e., SpringCloud), where the GRU component is connected to a TensorFlow cluster that scales independently; the enhanced semantic querier uses the interface of existing applications for data exchange to avoid complicated logics and adaptation; the local KG builder accesses a lexical processing tool Jieba [4] to implement semantic operations such as word segmentation; the periodic update process interacts with graph database Neo4j [5], and decouples the IIL solver through database operations;

Resource access layer. AIServiceX adopts a typical distributed service architecture including analyzer, database and resource schedulers, and interacts with the KG model service layer through standard Restful interfaces;

Knowledge base layer. AIServiceX interacts with multiple knowledge bases through the unique adaptation of reflection services. All adaptation codes are not diffused to avoid abnormal propagation caused by linking interruption and inconsistent events;

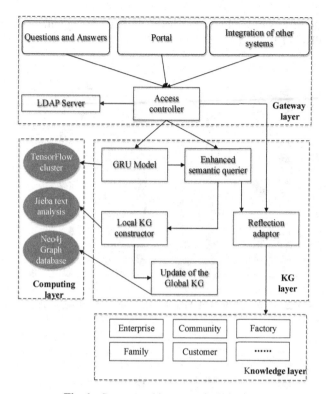

Fig. 1. System architecture of AIServiceX

5 Evaluation

5.1 Experiment Setting

We adopt a real business dataset of an e-commerce company. We pre-process and label the data, construct the KG, and then train the GRU model. Existing works often employ the precision, recall and F1 measure to evaluate methods, but they only count the number of binary problems. We extend the evaluation metrics by employing the matching degree of entities [11]. By counting queried answers, labeled correct answers, and the entities in each answer, we can accurately get the values of precision, recall and F1, respectively.

5.2 Heuristic Rules-Based Answer Ranking

We describe the similarities as "count" and "cos", and the random sort that returns the first result meeting the retrieval rules as "random". We sort the query results of entity assertions and KG on the test dataset to validate the effects. The experiment compares the results of QA-KG [11], CAN for QA [12] and CKB [7] We validate the performance improvement by comparing the output answers and the labeled correct answers with the distribution of entity assertions. Figure 2 shows that combining two heuristic rules can achieve better results than a single neural network or a dialogue model. Compared with single state-of-the-art methods, our heuristic rules can significantly improve the precision, recall and F1 indexes.

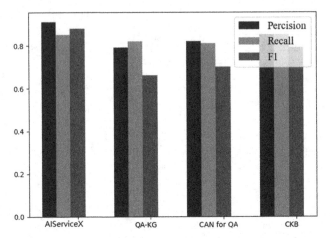

Fig. 2. Comparison with heuristic rules-based answer ranking

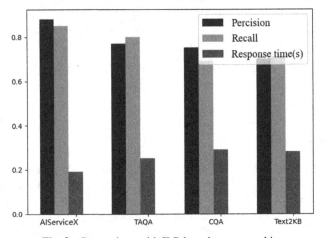

Fig. 3. Comparison with ILP-based answer ranking

5.3 Integer Linear Programming-Based Answer Ranking

The experiment compares the precision, recall and the average response time (seconds) of the full update strategy and the ILP strategy. Figure 3 shows the comparison of TAQA [1], CQA [2] and Text2KB [8]. After adopting different updating strategies, the ILP method brings a slight decrease of precision by 17%, and the decrease of average response time by 9%, which indicates that the space of answer retrieval is relatively concentrated, causing a low processing cost.

6 Related Work

Answering complex questions often involves the analysis of multiple entities and assertions, and requires as a long information retrieval chain. QUINT [6] automatically generates a question template to describe the mapping between questions and answers. CKB [7] defines a dialogue model collecting key elements to obtain accurate answers by guiding users to supplement semantic information. TAQA [1] proposes an N-tuple assertion model to deal with complex semantic constraints introduced by adjectives, verbs, and prepositions in complex questions. Seq2seq [9] employs the overlapping method to connect, duplicate and segment the questions and answers in large datasets. TEQUILA [10] proposes the detection and transformation method of a KG model to eliminate the time constraints of complex time-sensitive questions. Complex question-answering services have high cost and requires in-depth customization of applications, so these methods ought to spend much manual operations on customizing and training KG in the initialized period. AIServiceX accurately recognizes entities, automatically maps domain knowledge to the KG, and online updates the KG.

7 Conclusion

This paper proposes a KG based intelligent QA service integrating domain knowledge. We employ the GRU-based attention model to overcome the fuzziness of domain questions' expression, topic comparison-based enhanced semantic to construct the local KG and expand the knowledge of the global KG, and ILP update strategy to deal with the dynamic update of KG. AIServiceX can achieve a high precise answering results with a low response delay by accurately recognizing entities, automatically mapping domain knowledge to the KG, and online updating the KG. The experimental results show that AIServiceX improves the precision and decreases the response time.

Acknowledgment. This work is supported by National Key R&D Program of China (2018YFB1402900).

References

1. Yin, P., Duan, N., Kao, B., et al: Answering questions with complex semantic constraints on open knowledge bases. In: Proceedings of the 24th International on Conference on Information and Knowledge Management, pp. 1301–1310. ACM, New York (2015)
2. Chen, L., Jose, JM., Yu, H., et al.: A semantic graph based topic model for question retrieval in community question-answering. In: Proceedings of the Ninth International Conference on Web Search and Data Mining, pp. 287–296. ACM, New York (2016)
3. Savenkov, D., Agichtein, E.: When a knowledge base is not enough: Question-answering over knowledge bases with external text data. In: Proceedings of the 39th International SIGIR conference on Research and Development in Information Retrieval, pp. 235–244. ACM, New York (2016)
4. Sun, J.: 'Jieba' Chinese word segmentation tool, 25 August 2018. https://github.com/fxsjy/jieba. Accessed 20 May 2020

5. Lal, M.: Neo4j Graph Data Modeling. Packt Publishing Ltd, Birmingham (2015)
6. Abujabal, A., Yahya, M., Riedewald, M., et al.: Automated template generation for question-answering over knowledge graphs. In: Proceedings of the 26th International Conference on World Wide Web, pp. 1191–1200. ACM, New York (2017)
7. Wang, P., Ji, L., Yan, J., et al.: Learning to extract conditional knowledge for question-answering using dialogue. In: Proceedings of the 25th International on Conference on Information and Knowledge Management, pp. 277–286. ACM, New York (2016)
8. Savenkov, D., Agichtein, E.: When a knowledge base is not enough: Question answering over knowledge bases with external text data. In: Proceedings of the 39th International SIGIR conference on Research and Development in Information Retrieval, pp. 235–244. ACM, New York (2016)
9. Zhu, S., Cheng, X., Su, S., et al.: Knowledge-based question-answering by jointly generating, copying and paraphrasing. In: Proceedings of the Conference on Information and Knowledge Management, pp. 2439–2442. ACM, New York (2017)
10. Jia, Z., Abujabal, A., SahaRoy, R., et al.: TEQUILA: temporal question-answering over knowledge bases. In: Proceedings of the 27th International Conference on Information and Knowledge Management, pp. 1807–1810. ACM, New York (2018)
11. Huang, X., Zhang, J., Li, D., et al.: Knowledge graph embedding based question answering. In: Proceedings of the 12th International Conference on Web Search and Data Mining, pp. 105–113. ACM, New York (2019)
12. Li, H., Min, M.R., Ge, Y., et al.: A context-aware attention network for interactive question answering. In: Proceedings of the 23rd SIGKDD International Conference on Knowledge Discovery and Data Mining, pp. 927–935. ACM, New York (2017)

Review for Influence of 5G on Industry Internet

Yang Liu[1,2,3,4](✉), Liang-Jie Zhang[3,4], and Chunxiao Xing[1,2]

[1] Research Institute of Information Technology Beijing National Research, Center for Information Science and Technology, Tsinghua University, Beijing 100084, China
1491701161@qq.com

[2] Department of Computer Science and Technology Institute of Internet Industry, Tsinghua University, Beijing 100084, China

[3] National Engineering Research Center for Supporting Software of Enterprise Internet Services, Shenzhen 518057, China

[4] Kingdee Research, Kingdee International Software Group Company Limited, Shenzhen 518057, China

Abstract. In recent year, the downward pressure on the global economy is increasing, and the market is gradually changing. The urgent problem for entrepreneurs is how to keep their companies growing continuously. Industry Internet is a new direction that can help them by promoting business growth of enterprises. And the growth should be realized by exploring innovative business scenarios. The core of industry internet is not the internet, but the traditional industry. It forms the industry value chain through the mutual connection of traditional industries. The enterprises in each link of the value chain will become more powerful because of their value-added data. This paper solves several key problems in the development of enterprises: what economic era are they in? What is industry internet? How does industry Internet empower enterprises? How can 5G related technologies help traditional industries transform into industry internet?

Keywords: 5G · Industry internet · Digital economy · Business scenario

1 Introduction

Industry Internet is an industry ecology formed by remolding and transforming the industrial chain and internal value chain of each vertical industry. It is a new economic form, which makes full use of the Internet to integrate and optimize production resources, deeply integrates the Internet and traditional industries, and ultimately improves the productivity of the country. However, we are now in the era of consumer internet, existing many barriers in the transformation of enterprises to industry internet. Consumer internet regards consumers as the main body [1], and improves the consumption experience of individual users through e-commerce platform, while industry internet takes producers as the main body, with the purpose of connecting upstream and downstream industries, connecting intelligent devices of enterprise, and empowering different enterprises through industrial internet platform [2]. Since their service objects are different, enterprises need to constantly consolidate and accumulate their own industry insight,

© Springer Nature Switzerland AG 2020
J. E. Ferreira et al. (Eds.): SERVICES 2020, LNCS 12411, pp. 93–100, 2020.
https://doi.org/10.1007/978-3-030-59595-1_8

resource integration, platform empowerment, technology realization and operation management as well as other core capabilities to successfully realize the industry internet transformation [3]. This fundamental difference also leads to the fact that the industry internet not only cares about the links between people, but also needs to combine the technology of internet of things (IoT) [4] to realize the fine business process in industries.

5G related software provides the possibility to meet these needs. It includes the 5th generation mobile networks, internet of things, big data, artificial intelligence and other cutting-edge technologies. It provides the necessary conditions for enterprises to solve the fundamental technical problems faced by upgrading to the industrial internet, and is the basic guarantee for enterprises to obtain the core capabilities mentioned above. Therefore, analyzing and summarizing the influence of 5G related software technology on the development of industrial internet can help enterprises to maintain good growth in the current economic form. The rest of the article is summarized as follows. Section 2 gives an overview of digital economy ecosystem. In Sect. 3, this paper introduces 5G-based industry internet. Finally, Sect. 4 concludes the article.

2   An Overview of Digital Economy Ecosystem

The core of industry internet is industry, and the development of industry and economy is always inseparable. The integration of digital technology and traditional industry has changed the production way in enterprises and commodity trading mode in society, bringing people into the era of digital economy [5]. It refers to an economy that is based on digital computing technologies, and it is also called the internet Economy, the New Economy or Web Economy [6]. Web technology brings us to the era of digital economy 1.0, mobile internet brings digital economy 2.0, and industry internet brings digital economy 3.0 (see Table 1).

Table 1. Three stages in digital economy.

Digital economy	Infrastructure	Main features
1.0	Web	E-business, E-commerce
2.0	Cloud Computing	Business as Services, Mobile E-commerce
3.0	5G related technologies	Data value chain, Industrial value chain

2.1   Digital Economy 1.0

In the context of digital economy 1.0, traditional industries have basically realized digitalization [7]. Three major industries, agriculture, service industry and manufacturing industry, have established basic digital infrastructure [8]. In this era, it is mainly through web technology to change the way of production and commodity trading, to move the traditional offline business to the internet, to promote the sales of commodities through e-commerce platform [9, 10], and to improve the production efficiency through digital equipment, just as summarized in Table 1. The best example of digital economy 1.0 is to buy clothes and books online.

2.2 Digital Economy 2.0

We are now in the era of digital economy 2.0. Different from the former era, cloud computing is the infrastructure. The changes it brings to the industry development are service-oriented business and mobile e-commerce. Service-oriented business refers to turning customer relationship management, marketing and other general processes into repeatable digital services, and then presenting them in SaaS layer (software as a service). SaaS is the foundation of mobile Internet, and also spawned mobile e-commerce. Now, E-commerce based on mobile internet has become the most prominent feature of digital economy 2.0 (see Table 1).

Mobile internet generates big data [11]. After data aggregation, we can capitalize it and use this data asset to create new value again, which is what technology of big data does. In the future, we will use the data generated by one industry to other different industries, such as applying the data of intelligent manufacturing industry to the financial industry, which is the innovation of business scenario, the era of digital economy 3.0.

3 Digital Economy 3.0

3.1 Basic Concept

The most significant feature of digital economy 3.0 is data value chain and industrial value chain formed on 5G related technologies (see Table 1). In those chains, upstream and downstream enterprises of the industry are linked together, data flows efficiently across industries, and that is the vision of the industry internet.

5G related technologies include some cutting-edge technologies. 5G is the basis of internet of everything [12], internet of things generate big data [13], big data is analyzed by artificial intelligence to expand new business scenarios for enterprises [14], and block-chain secure those scenarios [15]. Innovative intelligent products are the product of the comprehensive application of these new technologies, and also the product of cross enterprise cooperation. In this ecosystem generated by the Innovation scenario, people and things, things and things are all interrelated, data is given new value in the flow, and the market value of related enterprises will increase. So, what problems need to be solved to meet the new economic era?

3.2 Obstacles to the Development of Industry Internet

As mentioned in the introduction Section, the formation of industry internet makes the digital economy upgrade. So the key problems lay in industry internet, such as how to improve equipment connection ability, break the limitations of industrial thinking, and integrate enterprise resources in a wide range.

- Equipment connection ability. In the IoT environment, the number of intelligent devices that need to be connected to the network is increasing rapidly. How to improve the connection ability of the device and the high concurrent access ability of the system is an urgent problem. 5G technology gives us an optimistic future.
- Barriers to industrial thinking. The industrial thinking of large-scale production has shown its disadvantages, that is, it is not conducive to the personalized production requirements and the digital transformation of enterprises. Industrial Internet thinking is the inevitable trend.
- Difficulties in integrating resources across enterprises. In order to make multiple enterprises work together efficiently, all kinds of resources in the product cycle must be integrated together to optimize the product design, production, logistics, marketing and other related aspects by using the industrial Internet platform.

3.3 Solutions for Developing Industry Internet

5G is the key technology to break down the barriers to the development of industry internet, which solves the problems of interconnection of everything and efficient flow of data (see Fig. 1). Device connecting service, radio transmission service, data storage and processing service constitute 5G-based service flow, the key ingredient of which is data flow. It promotes cooperation among enterprises, combination of upstream-downstream resources, efficient production and trading.

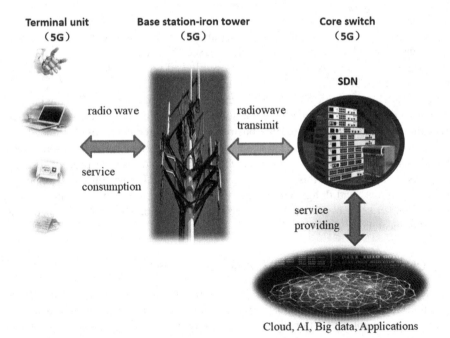

Fig. 1. 5G-based service flow

How can 5G improve equipment connection ability? It is a universal connector that can connect various terminals and services. Number of connected devices in the same area can be improved 100 times than 4G, and data transmission speed is 100 times faster than 4G (20 GB/s). In this way, various intelligent devices and business systems can be connected with each other through 5G message platform. 5G is like contact lenses. Its time delay in communication is only about 0.1 ms, which shortens the distance between users and service providers. 5G can reconstruct the value chain. With the support of 5G technology, the cooperation between enterprises is closer, the space of business innovation is larger, and the new value chain is easier to produce.

How to break the barriers of industrial thinking? The core of industry internet is to empower enterprises through digital transformation and provide solutions cross industry guided by services. Therefore, the solution of industry internet is designed around the service life cycle (see Fig. 2). The life cycle consists of six components: services consulting, services design, services development, services delivery, services operations and services management. By designing solutions around this life cycle, different departments or organizations are linked together. Data will flow when services are conducted between the two components, thus forming a data value chain.

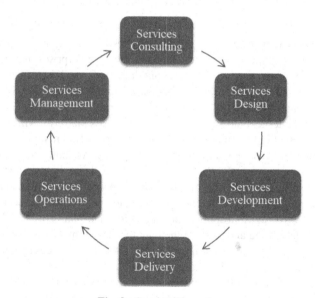

Fig. 2. Service life cycle

In the era of digital economy 3.0, data is an asset. It flows between different phases of service life cycle and will be given new value (see Fig. 3). UGC is short for used, generated and conducted. In the process of business interactions, data are used, generated and conducted. Value of data will continue to increase when data flow through different organizations. The recreated data will finally flow back to the whole data system. This value chain points out the direction of exploring new business model in the new economic era. Therefore, the essence of the digital economy 3.0 is data value-added services, and the data-driven economy.

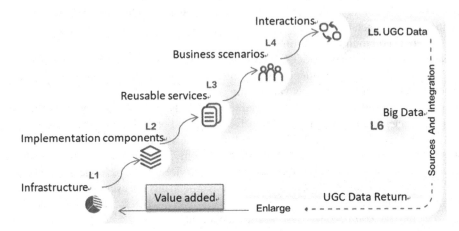

Fig. 3. Data value chain of digital economy 3.0

How to break through the barriers of enterprise resource integration? Industrial Internet is a platform to connect upstream and downstream enterprises and integrate various resources efficiently. Producers, sellers and logistics enterprises can carry out their own business around this platform. The industrial Internet platform will promote the development of enterprises in the direction of digitalization and intelligence.

The industrial internet platform is an open data access platform, which can integrate resources in various fields, promote rapid connectivity between suppliers and demanders, and optimize the resource allocation of enterprises. As shown in Fig. 4, it consists of four parts, edge layer, IaaS, PaaS and SaaS. Edge layer is to connect intelligent devices by using 5G networks, IaaS provides cloud computing function, PaaS integrates software developing tools or intelligent algorithm models and SaaS presents new opportunities for business design and application innovation. The platform can help enterprises collect massive data, store and analyze the data through digital technology. It links the resources of various industries and efficiently schedules the resources among enterprises. For example, in the manufacturing industry, the industrial internet platform can connect the staff, machines, workshops, enterprises and other subjects, and coordinate the design, development, production, sales and other aspects of products [16]. This platform can also be applied to other industry fields, such as oil and gas production, public utilities, large-scale industrial energy management and control center, to intelligentize the whole process of product design, production, commodity marketing, and logistics distribution. The way of internet + industrial manufacturing can enable different enterprises to combine into an industrial internet ecosystem cross industry, and further develop the industry ecosystem. It will form a deep integration of the new generation of information technology and manufacturing industry, and serve for China's intelligent manufacturing.

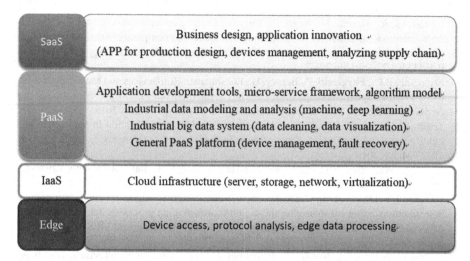

Fig. 4. Solution for industrial internet platform

4 Conclusions

This article introduces the background of industry internet and its relationship with digital economy, analyses the obstacles it encounters in the development process, presents how 5G related technologies contribute to forming industry internet, and puts forward solutions to overcome those obstacles. Conclusion is that, in the new economic situation, if enterprises want to survive and become more powerful, they must actively embrace the industry internet. Leading manufacturing enterprises need to combine 5G related technologies to build industrial internet platform, and use the platform to connect upstream and downstream enterprises. Other relevant enterprises need to actively complete digital transformation and access the industrial internet platform. In that way, all the enterprises associated with one specific business scenario can be linked into a value chain. However, there are still many problems to be solved in exploring innovative scenarios and making use of the industrial internet platform to implement those scenarios, for example, how to combine 5G technology to automatically discover smart devices and services nearby, how to ensure data security when exchanging data between different companies. These aspects are needed to be further studied in the field of industry internet.

References

1. Zhu, F., Li, G.: Study on security of electronic commerce information system. In: International Conference on Artificial Intelligence, Management Science and Electronic Commerce AIMSEC, 8–10 August 2011
2. Zhang, Y., Tao, F., Liu, Y., Zhang, P., Cheng, Y., Zuo, Y.: Long/short-term utility aware optimal selection of manufacturing service composition toward industrial internet platforms. IEEE Trans. Ind. Inform. **15**(6), 3712–3722 (2019). ISSN: 1551-3203

3. De Carolis, A., Macchi, M., Negri, E., Terzi, S.: Guiding manufacturing companies towards digitalization a methodology for supporting manufacturing companies in defining their digitalization roadmap. In: International Conference on Engineering, Technology and Innovation ICE/ITMC, 27–29 June 2017

4. hAnnaidh, B.O., Fitzgerald, P., Berney, H., Lakshmanan, R.: Devices and sensors applicable to 5G system implementations. In: IEEE MTT-S International Microwave Workshop Series on 5G Hardware and System Technologies IMWS-5G, 30–31 August 2018

5. Traub, M., Vögel, H.-J., Sax, E., Streichert, T., Härri, J.: Digitalization in automotive and industrial systems. In: Design, Automation & Test in Europe Conference & Exhibition DATE, 19–23 March 2018

6. Barua, A., Whinston, A.B., Yin, F.: Value and productivity in the Internet economy. Computer **33**(5), 102–105 (2000)

7. Ershova, T.V., Hohlov, Y.E., Shaposhnik, S.B.: Methodology for digital economy development assessment as a tool for managing the digital transformation processes. In: Eleventh International Conference Management of Large-Scale System Development MLSD, 1–3 October 2018

8. Vorobieva, D., Kefeli, I., Kolbanev, M., Shamin, A.: Architecture of digital economy. In: International Congress on Ultra Modern Telecommunications and Control Systems and Workshops ICUMT, 5–9 November 2018

9. Zuo, W., Hua, Q.: The application of web data mining in the electronic commerce. In: International Conference on Intelligent Computation Technology and Automation, 12–14 January 2012

10. Verma, S., Patel, K.: Importance of heuristic algorithms for ontology based search of product in mobile-commerce. In: International Conference on Inventive Systems and Control ICISC, 19–20 January 2018

11. Jiang, W., Wang, Y., Jiang, Y., Chen, J., Xu, Y., Tan, L.: Research on mobile internet mobile agent system dynamic trust model for cloud computing. China Commun. **16**(7), 174–194 (2019)

12. Liu, M., Mao, Y., Leng, S., Mao, S.: Full-duplex aided user virtualization for mobile edge computing in 5G networks. IEEE Access **6**, 2996–3007 (2017). ISSN: 2169-3536

13. Chettri, L., Bera, R.: A comprehensive survey on Internet of Things (IoT) toward 5G wireless systems. IEEE Internet Things J. **7**(1), 16–32 (2020). ISSN: 2327-4662

14. Akpakwu, G.A., Silva, B.J., Hancke, G.P., Abu-Mahfouz, A.M.: A survey on 5G networks for the Internet of Things: communication technologies and challenges. IEEE Access **6**, 3619–3647 (2017). ISSN: 2169-3536

15. Miller, D.: Blockchain and the Internet of Things in the industrial sector. IT Profess. **20**(3), 15–18 (2018). ISSN: 1520-9202

16. Li, Z., Zhou, X., Qin, Y.: A survey of mobile edge computing in the industrial internet. In: International Conference on Information, Communication and Networks ICICN, 24–26 April 2019

A Fuzzy AHP and TOPSIS Approach for Web Service Selection

Sandile T. Mhlanga[iD], Manoj Lall[✉], and Sunday O. Ojo[✉]

Tshwane University of Technology, Soshanguve, South Campus, Pretoria, South Africa
{MhlangaST,LallM,OjoSO}@tut.ac.za

Abstract. Multi criteria decision making (MCDM) model is proposed for determining the most suitable web service from a collection of functionally-equivalent web services with different non-functional properties. This paper presents an evaluation approach that combines fuzzy analytic hierarchy process (AHP) and Technique for Order Preference by Similarity to an Ideal Solution (TOPSIS) to solve the MCDM selection problems with conflicting criteria. Fuzzy AHP method determines subjective weights by dealing with vagueness and uncertainty in subjective user's judgment while, TOPSIS algorithm ranks the different alternatives. A numerical example is based on a real-world dataset is presented to illustrate the procedural matters of the web service selection model. The numerical results show that the proposed approach can effectively select an appropriate web service based on user preference. *WeatherStationService* performed better than other web services under the selected QoS requirements.

Keywords: Web services · Web services selection · Quality of service · Multi-criteria decision making · Fuzzy AHP · TOPSIS

1 Introduction

With the growth of the number of published web services, many offer similar functionality but different in non-functional properties (quality of service) [1]. A Web services is a software components available on the Web (through a URI), communicating through XML messages over an Internet transport protocol and whose capabilities and modus operandi are described in XML [2, 3]. Web service can be categorized as set of actions that are reachable with open XML standards like SOAP, UDDI and WSDL. Web service framework is categorized in to three main components: Service provider: The service provider develops the service and makes it accessible on the Internet for the users, Service requester: The service requestor is any end user of the web service [4]. The requestor consumes the already accessible web service returned by the service provider. Service registry is a centralized directory of web services that maintains the information about new and existing services [5, 6] as shown in Fig. 1.

The problem of selecting a suitable candidate web service from a pool of web services offering similar functions is considered as a MCDM problem [7]. According to [8] the only differentiating factor between similar web services may be their quality of service

© Springer Nature Switzerland AG 2020
J. E. Ferreira et al. (Eds.): SERVICES 2020, LNCS 12411, pp. 101–111, 2020.
https://doi.org/10.1007/978-3-030-59595-1_9

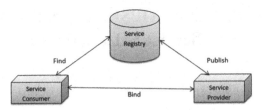

Fig. 1. Architecture for web service framework

(QoS), which are the quality aspect of a web service such as response time, availability, throughput, reliability and success ability [9]. Unfortunately, the QoS obtained from service descriptor (WSDL) or service providers (UDDI) do not reflect the real quality of these web services, they differ from a user to another, from a context to another and change dynamically in time according to several parameters [1, 4].

In view of this challenge, this study proposes a web service selection (WSS) hybrid model based on the combination of fuzzy AHP and TOPSIS. The AHP method, initially introduced by Saaty [34] is an effective technique for solving complex decision problems. AHP method represents a decision problem by a hierarchical organization reflecting the interactions between several components of the problem, then using pairwise comparison judgments to identify and evaluate the relative importance of criteria [35]. However, AHP method has some shortcoming due to its ineffectiveness when applied to an ambiguous problem with a high uncertainty [26]. Therefore several researchers such as [7, 24–28, 30] introduce fuzzy logic into the pairwise comparison of the AHP to compensate and deal with this type of fuzzy decision problem. In this paper fuzzy AHP is used to compute the weights of criteria. TOPSIS technique is that is utilized to rank the different alternative based on the computed weights. The basic principle of TOPSIS is that the selected alternative should have the shortest distance from the ideal solution and the farthest distance from the negative-ideal solution [10].

The remaining part of the article is organized as follows: Related works is presented in Sect. 2. Next, the research methodology used in this study is explained in Sect. 3. This is followed by results and discussion in Sect. 4, and lastly, the conclusions in Sect. 5.

2 Related Works

MCDM techniques are very beneficial in assisting decision makers in wide range of circumstances such as a multi-criteria analysis of alternative-fuel buses for public transportation in Taiwan [11], multi criteria selection for a restaurant location in Taipei [12], performance evaluation of customer satisfaction in Turkish banking sector [13]. The common goal is to find an optimal solution from a list of alternatives based on multiple deciding criteria.

In the context of WSS, many MCDM methods have been employed in the selection process such as AHP which has been utilized by [7, 14, 15] as a ranking procedure in select the best web service. Similarly, a web service selection approach based on analytical network process (ANP) was proposed by [16]. In other studies [17, 18] TOPSIS ranking algorithm is used to determine the most suitable web service. A trust based service selection is recommended by [19] using fuzzy modified Vlsekriterjumska optimizacija I KOmpromisno Resenje (VIKOR) method. The Preference Ranking and Organization METHod for Enrichment Evaluation (PROMETHEE) has been employed by [20, 21] as a web service selection approach.

The use of mixed methods as stated by [22] allows exploiting the advantages of every method and having better performance than using each method separately such as a web service selection model integrating AHP and VIKOR methods which was suggested by [33] the AHP method computed the weight of preference, while VIKOR technique ranked the alternatives. Another hybrid approach was proposed by [23] which combines AHP and reference ideal method (RIM). The AHP method is used to calculate the weights constraints assigned to QoS criteria while, RIM is used to rank the various alternatives. Similarly, a hybrid approached is presented by [4] for the selection of efficient web services. In this model, the AHP technique has been applied to calculate the individual weight value of non-functional parameters. Then, the Adaptive Ratio Assessment (ARAS) technique is used to rank web services. Relatedly, [1] suggested a hybrid approach to rank skyline web services, the subjective weight are computed using Fuzzy AHP from user opinions, while PROMETHEE method is used to rank the different alternatives.

In this paper Fuzzy AHP is used to evaluate the weight of criteria and TOPSIS method is applied to rank the various web services. In the weighting of subjective user judgment, pure AHP technique has some shortcomings. Human judgements are represented with exact (crisp) or ordinary data and also AHP method does not take into account the uncertainty associated with mapping of human judgment to a number by natural language. However, human preference is uncertain and decision maker might be reluctant or unable to assign exact numerical values to the comparison judgments [25, 26]. Therefore in this study, fuzzy extension of AHP is applied to overcome the shortcomings of traditional AHP method. To best of the authors knowledge, the integration of fuzzy AHP and TOPSIS methods have not utilized for WSS. The main contribution of this paper is to displaying the utilization of fuzzy AHP-TOPSIS methods for the WSS. The methodology applied in this paper explained in the next section.

3 Methodology

3.1 Fuzzy AHP Method

The AHP method with its fuzzy extension namely called Fuzzy AHP which is used to obtain more decisive judgments by prioritizing the web service selection criteria and weighting them in the presence of vagueness [7]. Fuzzy AHP can effectively handle both qualitative and quantitative data in the multiple criteria decision making problems. In this paper, triangular fuzzy numbers are utilized for the determination of one criterion over another by applying pairwise comparisons in the judgment matrix. The judgement matrix consists of fuzzy numbers and uses fuzzy arithmetic and fuzzy operations to determine the important weights for each criterion [7, 24, 25].

Table 1. Linguistic variables for pairwise comparison of each criterion [26]

Number	Linguistic variable	Scale of fuzzy number
9	Perfect	(9, 9, 9)
8	Absolute	(7, 8, 9)
7	Very good	(6, 7, 8)
6	Fairly good	(5, 6, 7)
5	Good	(4, 5, 6)
4	Preferably	(3, 4, 5)
3	Not bad	(2, 3, 4)
2	Weak advantage	(1, 2, 3)
1	Equal	(1, 1, 1)

Fuzzy AHP follows the following process [1, 24, 27–29]

Step 1: Decomposes the problem into a hierarchy.
Step 2: To determine relative weights, decision maker makes a pairwise comparison using Saaty's 1–9 preference scale. The pairwise data is organised in the form of fuzzy triangular numbers. The crisp values are replaced with triangular fuzzy numbers as shown in Table 1. If the decision maker cannot used the preference by form of fuzzy numbers, they can give preferences by linguistic terms, and use Table 1 for values, which can easily derive the corresponding fuzzy numbers.
Step 3: Computer the weight by using geometric mean method.
Step 4: Compute the consistency ratio (CR) to check the consistency of the decision matrix. If CR is less than 0.1, then the pairwise comparison matrix is consistent and acceptable. The consistency index (CI) and consistency ration (CR) of the pairwise comparison matrix are computed using the following Eqs. (1) and (2)

$$CI = (\lambda_{max} - n)/(n - 1) \tag{1}$$

$$CR = CI/RI \tag{2}$$

Where CI is the consistency index, n is the order of the pairwise comparison matrix A, λ_{max} is the maximum eigenvalue, while the random index RI is the average CI value for random matrices.

3.2 TOPSIS Method

TOPSIS is a well-known MCDM method based on the idea that the best alternative must have the least geometric distance from the positive ideal solution, and on the other side the farthest geometric distance of the negative ideal solution [30]. The positive ideal solution reflects the best solution with the most beneficial and lowest cost between all the alternative, while the negative ideal solution represents the worst solution with the lowest benefits and high cost [31]. The process of carrying out TOPSIS approach consists of the following steps [10, 17, 30, 31]:

Step 1: Construct decision matrix. Assume there are m alternatives and n number of criteria. Then, decision matrix is constructed with m rows and n columns as shown below.

$$DM = \begin{bmatrix} x_{11} & \cdots & x_{1n} \\ \vdots & \ddots & \vdots \\ x_{m1} & \cdots & x_{mn} \end{bmatrix} \tag{3}$$

Step 2: Construct a normalized decision matrix: The matrix is normalized using the application of Eq. (4).

$$p_{ij} = \frac{x_{ij}}{\sqrt{\sum_{i=1}^{m} x_{ij}^2}} \tag{4}$$

Where $i = 1, 2, \ldots, m$; $j = 1, 2, \ldots, n$ and x_{ij} is a crisp Value.

Step 3: Calculate the weighted normalized decision matrix. The weighted normalized matrix is generated by multiplying the normalized matrix with criteria weight. Equation (5) is applied in this stage.

$$v_{ij} = w_j \cdot p_{ij} \tag{5}$$

$$i = 1, 2, \ldots, m; \ j = 1, 2, \ldots, n$$

and w_j represents weight of jth criteria obtained by Fuzzy AHP method.

Step 4: Determine the ideal and negative-ideal solution

$$\begin{aligned} A^* &= \{v_1^*, \ldots, v_n^*\} \\ &= \left\{ \left(\max_j v_{ij} \middle| i \in I' \right), \left(\min_j v_{ij} \middle| i \in I'' \right) \right\}, \end{aligned} \tag{6}$$

$$\begin{aligned} A^- &= \{v_1^-, \ldots, v_n^-\} \\ &= \left\{ \left(\min_j v_{ij} \middle| i \in I' \right), \left(\max_j v_{ij} \middle| i \in I'' \right) \right\}, \end{aligned}$$

where I' is associated with the benefit criteria, and I'' is associated with non-benefit criteria.

Step 5: Calculate the separation measure, using the n-dimensional Euclidean distance. The separation of each alternative from the ideal solution is given as

$$D_j^* = \sqrt{\sum_{i=1}^{n} (v_{ij} - v_i^*)^2}, \quad j = 1, \ldots, J. \tag{7}$$

Similarly, the separation from the negative-ideal solution is given as

$$D_j^- = \sqrt{\sum_{i=1}^{n}\left(v_{ij} - v_i^-\right)^2}, \quad j = 1, \ldots, J. \tag{8}$$

Step 6: Calculate the relative closeness to the ideal solution. The relative closeness of the alternative a_j with respect to A^* is defined as

$$C_j^* = D_j^- \big/ \left(D_j^* + D_j^-\right), \quad j = 1, \ldots, J. \tag{9}$$

Step 7: Lastly, rank the preference order of alternatives by comparing C_j^* values; the best alternative is the one with the highest score of C_j^*

4 Experimental Example

The study uses five real – world web services: Cweather, PluralsightWeather, DOTS-FastWeather, WeatherStationService, and GlobalWeather. These web services and their measurements were obtained from quality of web service (QWS) dataset [32]. Response time, Availability, Throughput, Successability, and Reliability are the QoS parameters utilized as evaluation criteria in the selection process. Fuzzy AHP computes the weights, while TOPSIS ranks the different alternatives.

4.1 Calculation of the Criteria Weights Using Fuzzy AHP

Fuzzy AHP method is utilized to compute the criteria weights which are used during the selection process.

The service consumer enters preferences. A pairwise comparison matrix is generated using Saaty's 1–9 preference scale. The pairwise comparison matrix in Table 2 shows the user preference which have been captured.

Table 2. Pairwise comparison matrix

	RT	A	T	S	R
Response Time (RT)	1.00	0.33	2.00	0.50	0.25
Availability (A)	3.00	1.00	5.00	1.00	2.00
Throughput (T)	0.50	0.50	1.00	0.50	0.33
Success-ability (S)	2.00	1.00	2.00	1.00	0.50
Reliability (R)	4.00	0.50	3.00	2.00	1.00

The using fuzzy relative scale of importance shown in Table 1, a fuzzified pairwise comparison matrix is created by substituting the crisp number with a triangular fuzzy number. Table 3 illustrates a fuzzified pairwise comparison matrix where crisp numeric values have been replaced with fuzzy numbers.

Table 3. Fuzzified pairwise comparison matrix

	RT	A	T	S	R
Response Time (RT)	(1, 1, 1)	(0.25,0.33,0.5)	(1, 2, 3)	(0.33, 0.5, 1)	(0.2,0.25, 0.33)
Availability (A)	(2, 3, 4)	(1, 1, 1)	(4, 5, 6)	(1, 1, 1)	(1, 2, 3)
Throughput (T)	(0.33,0.5,1)	(0.16,0.2, 0.25)	(1, 1, 1)	(0.33,0.5, 1)	(0.25,0.33, 0.5)
Success-ability (S)	(1, 2, 3)	(1, 1, 1)	(1, 2, 3)	(1, 1, 1)	(0.33,0.5, 1)
Reliability (R)	(3, 4, 5)	(0.33, 0.5, 1)	(2, 3, 4)	(1, 2, 3)	(1, 1, 1)

Once the fuzzified matrix is created, the geometric mean value and the weight for all criterions are computed. The computed weights are in fuzzy form which can be used in the WSS process or can be de-fuzzified to get crisp numerical values. Table 4 shows the weights in a fuzzy form, in crisp numeric for, and the normalized weight which will be used in the ranking process by TOPSIS technique.

Table 4. Geometric Mean values, Fuzzy weight, Crisp weight, and Normalized weights

	Weight in fuzzy form	Crisp weights	Normalized weight
Response Time	(0.06, 0.10, 0.20)	0.12	0.11
Availability	(0.20, 0.34, 0.55)	0.36	0.32
Throughput	(0.04, 0.08, 0.16)	0.09	0.08
Success-ability	(0.10, 0.20, 0.36)	0.22	0.20
Reliability	(0.15, 0.28, 0.54)	0.32	0.29
	Sum	1.12	1.00

4.2 Ranking Alternative Using TOPSIS

Once the weights of the various QoS criterion have been computed, TOPSIS technique is applied to calculate and ranking the different web services. The weights calculated using Fuzzy AHP are shown in Table 5 and are used as input in the ranking process.

A quality of web service (QWS) dataset used in this study contains 2 507 web services that exist on the web. Table 6 present five web services measurements that are considered in the selection process.

Table 5. Weights based on user preference

	Response time	Availability	Throughput	Success-ability	Reliability
Weights	0.11	0.32	0.08	0.2	0.29

Table 6. Web service attributes measurements from the QWS dataset [32]

	Response time	Availability	Throughput	Success-ability	Reliability
Cweather	49.43	42	10.6	43	73
PluralsightWeather	645	86	8	86	73
DOTSFastWeather	110.78	85	13.2	95	73
WeatherStationService	237	97	20.7	99	73
GlobalWeather	285	85	4.2	95	73

The web service attribute measurements are normalized using the application of Eq. (4). Table 7 illustrates the different web service measurement read from the QWS dataset after normalization.

Table 7. Normalized decision matrix

	Response time	Availability	Throughput	Success-ability	Reliability
Cweather	0.06	0.23	0.37	0.22	0.44
Pluralsight-Weather	0.85	0.47	0.28	0.44	0.44
DOTSFastWeather	0.14	0.46	0.46	0.49	0.44
WeatherStationService	0.31	0.53	0.73	0.51	0.44
GlobalWeather	0.37	0.46	0.14	0.49	0.44

The next step involves calculating the weighted normalized decision matrix. The weighted normalized decision matrix is computed using Eq. (5). Table 8 shows the weighted normalized decision matrix after applying Eq. (5).

For every criterion, the positive ideal (best) solution and the negative ideal (worst) solutions are defined. Thereafter, the Euclidean distance for each alternative from the ideal or the negative – ideal is also determined by applying Eqs. (7) and (8).

Calculating the relative closeness to the ideal solution is determined by applying Eq. (9). Lastly, the alternative with the highest *Pi* score is selected the best alternative. Figure 2 illustrates the separation of each alternative from the ideal solution (*Si* +), the separation from the negative-ideal solution (*Si*−) and the relative closeness to the ideal solution (*Pi*). WeatherStationService is ranked best, based on the *Pi* score.

Table 8. Weighted normalized decision matrix

	Response time	Availability	Throughput	Success-ability	Reliability
Cweather	0.01	0.07	0.03	0.04	0.12
Pluralsight-Weather	0.09	0.15	0.02	0.08	0.12
DOTSFastWeather	0.01	0.14	0.03	0.09	0.12
WeatherStationService	0.03	0.17	0.05	0.10	0.12
GlobalWeather	0.04	0.14	0.01	0.09	0.12

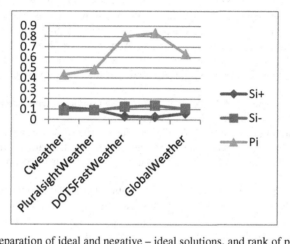

Fig. 2. Separation of ideal and negative – ideal solutions, and rank of preference

5 Conclusion

In this paper, related researchers were investigated with the focus on their strengths and shortcomings. A hybrid approach for WSS is presented. Although the data related to the weight is gathered from users, the fuzzy AHP method is applied for computation of criteria weights. Subsequently, the TOPSIS technique is utilized to rank the various web services based on the computed weights. To demonstrate how the proposed hybrid model works and how it can be applied on WSS, an example using QoS criteria and QWS dataset for web services (alternatives) measurements is provided. The result shows that WeatherStationService performed better than other web search services under the selected QoS requirements. The model can effectively rank and select the best suitable web service. For future work, the comparison of the results obtained by our proposed model with another replicated study using other MCDM method, such as ELECTRE or PROMETHEE.

References

1. Ouadah, A., Hadjali, A., Nader, F., Benouaret, K.: SEFAP: an efficient approach for ranking skyline web services. J. Ambient Intell. Hum. Comput. **10**(2), 709–725 (2018). https://doi.org/10.1007/s12652-018-0721-7
2. Benatallah, B., Dijkman, R.M., Dumas, M., Maamar, Z.: Service-composition: concepts, techniques, tools and trends. In: Service-Oriented Software System Engineering: Challenges and Practices, pp. 48–67. IGI Global (2005)
3. Lall, M., van der Poll, J.A., Venter, L.M.: Towards a formal definition of availability of web services, pp. 154–165, 11–13 November 2012
4. Negi, N., Chandra, S.: A novel approach for efficient web service selection based on QoS parameters. Int. J. Adv. Stud. Sci. Res. **3** (2018)
5. Negi, N., Chandra, S.: Web service selection on the basis of QoS parameter. In: 2014 Seventh International Conference on Contemporary Computing (IC3), pp. 495–500 (2014)
6. Rajendran, T., Balasubramanie, P., Cherian, R.: An efficient WS-QoS broker based architecture for web services selection. Int. J. Comput. Appl. **1**, 79–84 (2010)
7. Kumar, R.R., Kumar, C.: An evaluation system for cloud service selection using fuzzy AHP. In: 2016 11th International Conference on Industrial and Information Systems (ICIIS), pp. 821–826 (2016)
8. Aljazzaf, Z.M., Capretz, M.A., Perry, M.: Trust-based service-oriented architecture. J. King Saud Univ.-Comput. Inf. Sci. **28**, 470–480 (2016)
9. Lall, M., Venter, L.M., Van der Poll, J.A.: Evaluating the second generation Web services specifications for satisfying non-functional requirements. In: E-Learn: World Conference on E-Learning in Corporate, Government, Healthcare, and Higher Education, pp. 1919–1929 (2010)
10. Opricovic, S., Tzeng, G.-H.: Compromise solution by MCDM methods: a comparative analysis of VIKOR and TOPSIS. Eur. J. Oper. Res. **156**, 445–455 (2004)
11. Tzeng, G.-H., Lin, C.-W., Opricovic, S.: Multi-criteria analysis of alternative-fuel buses for public transportation. Energy Policy **33**, 1373–1383 (2005)
12. Tzeng, G.-H., Teng, M.-H., Chen, J.-J., Opricovic, S.: Multicriteria selection for a restaurant location in Taipei. Int. J. Hosp. Manag. **21**, 171–187 (2002)
13. Dincer, H., Hacioglu, U.: Performance evaluation with fuzzy VIKOR and AHP method based on customer satisfaction in Turkish banking sector. Kybernetes **42**, 1072–1085 (2013)
14. Kumar, R.D., Zayaraz, G.: A QoS aware quantitative web service selection model. Int. J. Comput. Sci. Eng. **3**, 1534–1538 (2011)
15. Jozwiak, I., Kedziora, M., Marianski, A.: Service selection method with multiple probabilistic QoS attributes using probabilistic AHP. Int. J. Comput. Sci. Netw. Secur. **18**, 33–38 (2018)
16. Godse, M., Sonar, R., Mulik, S.: Web service selection based on analytical network process approach. In: 2008 IEEE Asia-Pacific Services Computing Conference, pp. 1103–1108 (2008)
17. Lo, C.-C., Chen, D.-Y., Tsai, C.-F., Chao, K.-M.: Service selection based on fuzzy TOPSIS method. In: 2010 IEEE 24th International Conference on Advanced Information Networking and Applications Workshops, pp. 367–372 (2010)
18. Joshi, S.S., Ramanaiah, O.: An integrated QoE and QoS based approach for web service selection. In: 2016 International Conference on ICT in Business Industry & Government (ICTBIG), pp. 1–7 (2016)
19. Alabool, H.M., Mahmood, A.K.: Trust-based service selection in public cloud computing using fuzzy modified VIKOR method. Aust. J. Basic Appl. Sci. **7**, 211–220 (2013)
20. Karim, R., Ding, C., Chi, C.-H.: An enhanced PROMETHEE model for QoS-based web service selection. In: 2011 IEEE International Conference on Services Computing, pp. 536–543 (2011)

21. Purohit, L., Kumar, S.: A classification based web service selection approach. IEEE Trans. Serv. Comput. (2018)
22. Ouadah, A., Benouaret, K., Hadjali, A., Nader, F.: SkyAP-S3: a hybrid approach for efficient skyline services selection. In: 2015 IEEE 8th International Conference on Service-Oriented Computing and Applications (SOCA), pp. 18–25 (2015)
23. Serrai, W., Abdelli, A., Mokdad, L., Serrai, A.: Dealing with user constraints in MCDM based web service selection. In: 2017 IEEE Symposium on Computers and Communications (ISCC), pp. 158–163 (2017)
24. Güngör, Z., Serhadlıoğlu, G., Kesen, S.E.: A fuzzy AHP approach to personnel selection problem. Appl. Soft Comput. **9**, 641–646 (2009)
25. Durán, O., Aguilo, J.: Computer-aided machine-tool selection based on a Fuzzy-AHP approach. Expert Syst. Appl. **34**, 1787–1794 (2008)
26. Chou, Y.-C., Sun, C.-C., Yen, H.-Y.: Evaluating the criteria for human resource for science and technology (HRST) based on an integrated fuzzy AHP and fuzzy DEMATEL approach. Appl. Soft Comput. **12**, 64–71 (2012)
27. Çelik, P., Gök Kisa, A.C.: Fuzzy AHP-fuzzy promethee approach in evaluation of e-service quality: case of airline web sites. J. Int. Soc. Res. **10** (2017)
28. Brahma, A.K., Mitra, D.K.: Fuzzy AHP and fuzzy VIKOR approach modelling for flood control project selection. Int. J. Appl. Eng. Res. **14**, 3579–35889 (2019)
29. Jatoth, C., Gangadharan, G.R., Fiore, U., Buyya, R.: SELCLOUD: a hybrid multi-criteria decision-making model for selection of cloud services. Soft. Comput. **23**(13), 4701–4715 (2018). https://doi.org/10.1007/s00500-018-3120-2
30. Perçin, S., Aldalou, E.: Financial performance evaluation of Turkish airline companies using integrated fuzzy AHP fuzzy TOPSIS model. In: Uluslararası İktisadi ve İdari İncelemeler Dergisi (18. EYİ Özel Sayısı), pp. 583–598 (2018)
31. Kumar, R.R., Mishra, S., Kumar, C.: A novel framework for cloud service evaluation and selection using hybrid MCDM methods. Arab. J. Sci. Eng. **43**, 7015–7030 (2018). https://doi.org/10.1007/s13369-017-2975-3
32. Al-Masri, E., Mahmoud, Q.H.: Investigating web services on the world wide web. In: Proceedings of the 17th International Conference on World Wide Web, pp. 795–804 (2008)
33. Mhlanga, S.T., Lall, M., Ojo, S.O.: Web service selection model using a hybrid approach. Int. J. Eng. Appl. Sci. **15**(4), 948–955 (2020)
34. Pan, N.-F.: Fuzzy AHP approach for selecting the suitable bridge construction method. Autom. Constr. **17**(8), 958–965 (2008)
35. Boutkhoum, O., Hanine, M., Agouti, T., Tikniouine, A.: Selection problem of cloud solution for big data accessing: fuzzy AHP-PROMETHEE as a proposed methodology. J. Digit. Inf. Manag. **14**(6) (2016)

Author Index

Printed in the United States
By Bookmasters